How to Probate an Estate in Massachusetts

With Forms and Checklist

Richard A. Feigenbaum
Eleanor M. Uddo
Attorneys at Law

SPHINX PUBLISHING
Sphinx International, Inc.
1725 Clearwater-Largo Rd., S.
Post Office Box 25
Clearwater, FL 34617
Tel. (813) 587-0999
Fax (813) 586-5088

SPHINX®
is a registered trademark of Sphinx International, Inc.

> Note: The law changes constantly and is subject to different interpretations. It is up to you to check it thoroughly before relying on it. Neither the author nor the publisher guarantees the outcome of the uses to which this material is put.

First Edition, 1997

ISBN 1-57248-053-X
Library of Congress Catalog Number: 96-69196

Manufactured in the United States of America.

This publication is designed to provide accurate and authoritative information in regard to the subject matter covered. It is sold with the understanding that the publisher is not engaged in rendering legal, accounting or other professional services. If legal advice or other expert assistance is required, the service of a competent professional person should be sought.

-From a Declaration of Principles jointly adopted by a Committee of the American Bar Association and a Committee of Publishers.

Published by Sphinx Publishing, a division of Sphinx International, Inc., Post Office Box 25, Clearwater, Florida 34617-0025. This publication is available by mail for $19.95 plus $3.00 postage.

Table of Contents

Introduction 7

Using Self-help Law Books 8

Chapter 1   An Overview of Probate 9
   What is Probate?
   When is Probate Necessary?
   Types of Probate
   Types of Ownership of Property and How it Effects Probate
   Do You Need an Attorney?
   How to Find an Attorney
   Duty to Deliver the Will
   Proof of Lost or Misplaced Wills
   Procedure for Obtaining a Will Locked in a Safe Deposit Box
   Funeral Issues
   Anatomical Gifts
   Automobile Related Issues
   Small Estates
   What is a Voluntary Probate?
   What are the Legal Requirements?
   Who May Serve as Voluntary Executor or Voluntary Administrator?
   How to File for Appointment
   Filled in Forms 1 and 2

Chapter 2   Probate of the Large Estate — With a Will 17
   Probate When There is a Will
   Petition to Probate the Will
   Purpose of Petition to Probate Will
   Filing the Petition
         Last Will and Testament
         Death Certificate
         Bond
         Payment of Filing Fees
   The Citation
         Publishing the Citation
         Notices
         Return of Citation to Probate Court
   Filled in Forms 3-7

Chapter 3   Probate of a Large Estate — Without a Will 27
   Who May Serve as Administrator?
   Filing the Petition
         Death Certificate
         Bond

Payment of Filing Fees
The Citation
Publishing the Citation
Notices
Return of Citation to Probate Court
Filled in Forms 8-10

Chapter 4   **The Probate Bond** 33
Bond with Sureties
Bond without Sureties
Filled in Form 11

Chapter 5   **The Inventory** 37
Preparing the Inventory
Real Estate
Personal Estate
Bank Accounts and Investments
Publicly traded stocks and bonds
Closely Held Stock
Other Assets
Items Not Included

Chapter 6   **What to Do Once You Are Appointed** 39
Collecting Assets and Expenses
Closing Accounts and Collecting Assets
Bank Accounts
Closing Stock Brokerage Accounts
What Are the Rules for Paying Bills?
Do I Need an Identification Number for the Estate? / How Do I Get One?
What Do You Do with Estate Assets?
What Shouldn't You Do with Estate Assets
Insurance Benefits
Social Security Benefits
Filled in Forms 12-15

Chapter 7   **Dealing with Real Estate** 47
General
Valuation
Who Owns the Real Estate?
Selling the Real Estate
License to Sell Real Estate
Estate Tax Issues
Massachusetts Estate Taxes
Federal Estate Taxes
Purchase and Sale Agreement
Filled in Forms 16 and 17

Chapter 8   Debts and Expenses / Claims of Creditors 55
        General
        Enforcement of Claims Against the Estate

Chapter 9   Estate Taxes 57
        In General
        Federal Estate Taxes
        Massachusetts Estate Taxes

Chapter 10   Non-Resident Decedents/Ancillary Administration 59

Chapter 11   Closing the Probate Docket - Probate Accounts 61
        Requirements
        Contents and Format of Accounts
        Schedule A - Receipts
        Schedule B - Expenditures
        Schedule C - Remaining Balance
        Filing and Allowance of Accounts
            Fees
            Filing Requirements
            Steps for Allowance
                Mailing
                Publication
                The Return
        Charities
        Guardian Ad Litem
        Documents Necessary to Present an Account for Allowance
            Military Affidavit
            Estate Tax Closing Letter
            Judgment for Use by the Probate Court
            Written Assents
            Transmittal Letter
        Contesting an Account
        Appeal of Allowed Account
        Filled in Forms 18 and 19

Chapter 12   Payment of Legacies / Distribution of Intestate Property 73
        Payment of Legacies
        Real Estate
        Payment of Legacies to Minors
        Filled in Form 20

Glossary 77

Appendix A Probate Checklist 79

Appendix B Forms 83

    Form 1   Voluntary Executor/Executrix
    Form 2   Voluntary Administration
    Form 3   Probate of Will with/without Sureties
    Form 4   Declination
    Form 5   General Assent
    Form 6   Appointment of Agent
    Form 7   Military Affidavit
    Form 8   Administration with/without Sureties
    Form 9   Probate of Will — Administration with the Will Annexed
               with/without Sureties
    Form 10 Special Administration
    Form 11 Bond
    Form 12 Affidavit of Domicile
    Form 13 Notice to Bank
    Form 14 Notice to Mutual Funds Co.
    Form 15 Application for employer I.D. Number
    Form 16 Affidavit Regarding Federal Estate Taxes
    Form 17 Sale of Real Estate
    Form 18 Account
    Form 19 Judgment
    Form 20 Receipt of Distribution

Index 127

Introduction

This book has been designed to assist in the unraveling of the confusion surrounding Massachusetts Probate Law and Practice. In its simplest form, Massachusetts probate law has not changed in the last several hundred years. In fact, the probate court forms used today have been in use by the Massachusetts Probate Courts since the early 1800s. The changes that have taken place relate to the role that the probate court plays in the family after the death of an individual. Due to the expense and public nature of the probate process, more and more people include "probate avoidance" as a goal in planning their estate.

The text which follows is divided into two categories. Probate where there is a will, and probate where there is no will. Whether there is or is not a will, the probate process, and its many requirements and details, are virtually the same. Once you have identified which of the two main areas you need to review, the balance of the book expands on the details of the probate process you are about to undertake.

Using Self-Help Law Books

Whenever you shop for a product or service, you are faced with a variety of different levels of quality and price. In deciding what to buy, you make a cost/value analysis on the basis of your willingness to pay and the quality you desire.

When buying a car, you decide whether you want transportation, comfort, status, or sex appeal, and you decide among such choices as a Neon, a Lincoln, a Rolls Royce, or a Porsche. Before making a decision, you usually weigh the merits of each against the cost.

When you get a headache, you can take a pain reliever such as aspirin or you can go to a medical specialist for a neurological examination. Given this choice, most people, of course, take a pain reliever, since it costs only pennies, whereas a medical examination costs hundreds of dollars and takes a lot of time. This is usually a logical choice because rarely is anything more than a pain reliever needed for a headache. But in some cases a headache may indicate a brain tumor, and failing to go to a specialist right away can result in complications. Should everyone with a headache go to a specialist? Of course not, but people treating their own illnesses must realize that they are betting on the basis of their cost/value analysis of the situation, that they are taking the most logical option.

The same cost/value analysis must be made in deciding to do one's own legal work. Many legal situations are very simple, requiring a simple form and no complicated analysis. Anyone with a little intelligence and a book of instructions can handle the matter simply.

But there is always the chance that there is a complication involved that only a lawyer would notice. To simplify the law into a book like this, several legal cases often must be condensed into a single sentence or paragraph. Otherwise, the book would be several hundred pages long and too complicated for most people. However, this simplification necessarily leaves out many details and nuances that would apply to special or unusual situations. Also, there are many ways to interpret most legal questions. Your case may come before a judge who disagrees with the analysis of our author.

Therefore, in deciding to use a self-help law book and to do your own legal work, you must realize that you are making a cost/value analysis and deciding that the chance that your case will not turn out to your satisfaction is outweighed by the money you will save by doing it yourself. Most people handling their own simple legal matters never have a problem, but occasionally people find that it ended up costing them more to have an attorney straighten out the situation than it would have if they had hired an attorney to begin with. Keep this in mind while handling your case, and be sure to consult an attorney if you feel you might need further guidance.

Chapter 1
An Overview of Probate

What is Probate?

Probate is a legal process designed to assist in administering the assets owned by a decedent at the time of his or her death. Specifically, the probate court assists the person named to take charge of the decedent's assets (the estate fiduciary) so that the decedent's wishes as expressed in his or her last will and testament can be followed. As will be discussed in great length throughout these materials, the only assets which fall subject to the probate process are assets which are in a decedent's name alone at the time of death and assets which are made payable to the decedent's estate (such as insurance).

When is Probate Necessary?

Probate is necessary any time a resident of the Commonwealth of Massachusetts passes away owning assets in the person's name alone. In addition to assets owned individually, any real estate which is owned as a tenant in common would also fall subject to the probate court process.

Nonresidents are also subject to a Massachusetts probate if they own property in Massachusetts at the time of death.

Types of Probate

If the assets subject to probate are less than $15,000 excluding an automobile, a simple procedure called a "Voluntary Probate" can be used to settle the estate. An explanation of this procedure is included at the end of this chapter.

For larger estates the procedure will depend on whether there is a will. For probates with a will the explanation is covered by chapter 2. For probates where there is no will, the procedure is covered by chapter 3. The rest of the chapters in this book apply to both types of probate.

Types of Ownership of Property and How it Effects Probate

Since only those assets in a decedent's name alone at the time of death are subject to the probate process, a careful review of the assets owned by a decedent, as well as the form of ownership of the assets, is extremely important. If the decedent owned an asset as a joint owner with another individual where the joint ownership provided for a right of survivorship, then the asset would not be part of the probate process. The most typical examples of this joint ownership are joint ownership of real estate between spouses ("known as husband and wife as tenants by the entirety") and joint ownership of assets as "joint ownership with rights of survivorship". In each of these cases upon the death of one of the joint owners the property passes instantly, by operation of law, to the survivor. Since the asset instantly passes to another individual it is not treated as though it were owned by the decedent in his name alone and therefore does not become part of the probate process.

One form of joint ownership does require the asset be listed as part of the probate estate. This form of ownership is known as "tenancy in common". In a tenancy in common the two joint owners each own their respective halves of the property such that upon the passing of one of the co-owners the property does not pass to the survivor. For this reason the asset is treated as though the decedent's portion of the asset was owned in his or her name alone.

Do You Need an Attorney?

There is no statutory requirement in Massachusetts that a legal representative of an estate be represented by an attorney. In the "voluntary" forms of probate (Voluntary Administration and Voluntary Executor) the process envisions no true, bonded representative being named for the estate. In these cases there is little or no need for legal counsel in preparing the necessary court documents. The only requirement in the filing of the "voluntary" petition is that the petition be witnessed by a notary.

For the more formal probate actions such as an Administration and a Probate of Will, the process is one of strict adherence to the mandates of the probate court in which the case is filed. There are cases where motions need to be made of the probate court, such as obtaining a License to Sell Real Estate, in which case it would be advisable to retain legal counsel.

As many probate actions are filed without the assistance of legal counsel, the clerks of the probate court have historically been inundated by requests for assistance in completing and filing the necessary probate documents. The Massachusetts Supreme Judicial Court has mandated that no officer or employee of the probate court may provide legal assistance while an employee of the court. The Registers of most probate courts have taken the position that assistance in the preparation and filing of probate petitions and documents constitutes legal services. As such, the clerks and registers at each probate court cannot and will not assist in completing probate documents. They will however tell you what errors have been made in documents you may be attempting to file and by trial and error you can succeed in filing the appropriate paperwork.

How to Find an Attorney

Word of mouth, as always, is the basis upon which most people select an attorney. Other approaches to securing legal counsel might be to contact the Massachusetts Bar Association or the Boston Bar Association which maintain lawyer referral lists categorized by area of practice.

Selecting legal counsel should be no different than any other consumer transaction and, accordingly, the interested party should interview several attorneys to determine whether the attorney has sufficient expertise in the area and the type of legal practice that will allow for a smooth and cost effective process. Each attorney should be questioned about the cost of his or her legal services as well as the cost for paralegal, secretaries, etc. As is the case in most states, attorneys undertaking probate type matters tend to charge on an hourly basis and not as a percentage of the probate estate. While there are certain attorneys who will charge as a percentage of the estate the majority of attorneys charge by the hour. It would be wise to obtain a written fee agreement stipulating all terms and conditions of legal representation so that there will be no misunderstandings as to billing matters.

Duty to Deliver the Will

An overriding goal of the probate process is to be certain that all of the decedent's wishes are strictly adhered to as expressed in his or her will. For this reason Massachusetts General Law requires that a diligent search of the most recently executed will should always be made. Obvious locations for an original will would be the decedent's home or office, the attorney's office who prepared or is most likely to have prepared the will, the decedent's safe deposit box or the probate court in the county in which the decedent lived.

If more than one original will is discovered then the most recently executed valid will is the document that controls. For this reason people who revise and update their wills should be certain to destroy all documents pre-dating the new will to be certain that the wrong will is not discovered upon death. This confusion can be even greater when several wills are executed within a short period of time. Many will contests are centered on the validity of a particular will when several very similar wills have been executed by a decedent within a relatively short period of time.

Proof of Lost or Misplaced Wills

As a general proposition, only the original will of the decedent can be admitted to the probate court as a valid last will and testament. If a will is known to have existed but cannot be found the presumption is that the creator of the will chose to destroy or revoke it. It is possible to counter this argument with other evidence, however the evidence must create a circumstance that is "free from doubt". Photocopies or conformed copies of a will do not provide any better answer in that they too must overcome the presumption that the decedent chose to revoke or destroy the will.

Procedure for Obtaining a Will Locked in a Safe Deposit Box

If the last will and testament cannot be located elsewhere, then a search of the decedent's safe deposit box should be made. Until a legal representative of the estate has been appointed no one has the authority to enter the decedent's safe deposit box. Almost all banks have a procedure to allow a bank officer to open the safe deposit box for the limited purpose of determining whether the original will is in the safe deposit box. In the event the bank does not have such a process than a Petition for the Appointment of a Special Administrator would need to be brought to obtain court authority to enter the box.

As a first step the contract between the decedent and the bank in which the safe deposit box is maintained should be reviewed to determine that no other person has legal authority to sign on the box. Very often safe deposit boxes can be jointly owned or can have more than one signatory allowing access to the box.

The Department of Revenue in Massachusetts does not typically seal a safe deposit box after the death of the owner of the box. Unlike many other states, Massachusetts does not require the presence of a representative from the Department of Revenue at the time the box is opened and contents removed.

Funeral Issues

If a decedent left specific instructions about the nature and type of burial then these wishes should control even against objections of family members. If there are no directions for burial left by the decedent then the surviving spouse or, if there is no surviving spouse, the next of kin has legal possession of the body for burial. If there is no surviving spouse and the next of kin are minors then the legal guardians of the minors would exercise the right to arrange for the burial. A thorough search of the decedent's personal effects should be made to determine whether any burial arrangements have been made, to attempt to locate any cemetery deed, and to determine whether a burial contract has already been entered into and paid for on a prepaid basis.

Anatomical Gifts

Massachusetts law provides for a person at least 18 years of age and of sound mind to donate part or all of his or her body for transplantation, scientific purposes, etc.

Automobile Related Issues

The automobile which the decedent owned at the time of his death, provided that it is properly registered, continues to have a valid registration until the expiration date of the current registration period or until an executor is appointed and the vehicle is transferred or sold.

The insurance which the decedent had in place on the automobile remains in full force and allows blood relatives of the decedent to drive the vehicle and be fully insured until the estate representative has been appointed. Once the estate representative has been appointed that person is the only person who may operate the vehicle and be fully insured.

In instances where the automobile is registered in the decedent's name alone, Massachusetts provides for a simple process in which a surviving spouse may have the vehicle retitled in his or her name. For all intents and purposes Massachusetts is treating the solely registered and owned vehicle as though it were joint property. The surviving spouse would contact the Registry of Motor Vehicles and complete the necessary Surviving Spouse Affidavit and present a death certificate. The registration would then be issued in the name of the surviving spouse.

Small Estates

A Voluntary Probate, also known as a Voluntary Executor or a Voluntary Administration is a simplified form of Probate Administration which can be used when the decedent had a small amount of assets in his or her name alone. The Massachusetts Probate Court system acknowledges that small estates do not need to be put through the same formalities as a large estate. For this reason, the Probate Court rules allows for an informal probate process to administer small estates. A small estate is defined as any estate in which the value of assets in the decedent's name alone does not exceed $15,000.00. This $15,000.00 limit does not include the value of an automobile.

What are the Legal Requirements?

The legal requirements for an estate to qualify for the informal voluntary probate process are as follows:

1. The decedent must have lived in Massachusetts at the time of his or her death.

2. The decedent leaves behind an estate which consists entirely of personal property (bank accounts, stocks, bonds, personal assets, etc.) in the decedent's name alone. Under no circumstances can any portion of this be comprised of real estate.

3. The value of all assets in the decedent's name, excluding the value of any automobile, cannot exceed $15,000.00.

4. At least 30 days must have passed from the date of the decedent's death and no formal probate process has been filed with any probate court since the time of the decedent's death.

If all of the above requirements exist, then the estate may be probated using an informal process. The benefit to the informal process is that the entire process can often be completed within two weeks, thereby eliminating the lengthy time delay that so often accompanies a formal Probate Administration.

Who May Serve as Voluntary Executor or Voluntary Administrator?

If all of the requirements are satisfied, a Petition can be filed requesting the appointment of a Voluntary Executor or Voluntary Administrator. If the decedent had a will at the time of his death, then the Executor named in the will would be the person who would petition to be named Voluntary Executor. If the decedent did not have a will, then there is a short list of people who are eligible to request that they be appointed Voluntary Administrator. The approved list of people is as follows: surviving spouse, child, grandchild, parent, brother/sister, niece/nephew, aunt/uncle.

In each of these cases, as with anyone petitioning to be named in a fiduciary capacity in the Probate Court, only someone who has reached the legal age of 18 years of age may act in this capacity.

How do I File for Appointment?

To begin the process, the person who will be serving as the Voluntary Executor/Administrator will complete the appropriate form, Form CJ-P7A (Voluntary Executor/Executrix) or Form CJ-P7 (Voluntary Administration). (Completed forms follow as Form 1 and Form 2.)

Once the Petition is completed, the person requesting to serve must sign the document in front of a notary who will also sign the document affixing his or her seal. The petition is then filed with the Probate Court of the County of the decedent's residence at the time of his or her death. The cost for filing a Voluntary Petition is fifty ($50.00) dollars, which includes the cost of a certified copy of the Petition once it is allowed. The Petition must be filed with a certified copy of the death certificate and the original will if one exists. In approximately a week, the Probate Court will sign the petition and return a copy to the person named as petitioner. The document returned by the Court will have an embossed Court seal evidencing the allowance of the Petition and the Appointment of the person named. With this court document, the named Petitioner can undertake actions on behalf of the decedent's estate.

As with any fiduciary named by the Probate Court, the named Executor/Administrator must first collect all assets and pay all priority expenses. Priority expenses are the expenses of the funeral and last illness of the decedent and expenses of the Probate Administration. Once those are paid, any other debts of the decedent should be paid with the balance of assets being distributed with the terms of the will or to the heirs of the decedent if there is no will.

Petition for Voluntary Executor/Executrix

Purpose: Petition for Voluntary Executor/Executrix is utilized when the decedent's assets do not exceed $15,000.00, excluding the value of any automobile.

1) County of decedent's residence at time of death.

2) Name of decedent.

3) Domicile at date of death.

4) Date of death.

5) Name and address of Petitioner.

6) Status, i.e. relationship and status as executor/executrix.

7) Listing of all assets and estimated value (not to exceed $15,000.00 in total).

8) Listing of all heirs at law and joint owners of property.

9) Copy of the Petition along with the death certificate must be mailed to the Department of Public Welfare.

10) Signature line for Petitioner.

11) The signature of the petitioner must be notarized, with the notary affixing his/her seal to the document.

Form 1

Commonwealth of Massachusetts
The Trial Court
Probate and Family Court Department

(1) __Norfolk__ Division   Docket No. _____

Voluntary Executor/Executrix

Name of Decedent (2) __Steven J. Williams__
Domicile at Death (3) __42 Newmarket Street__ __Wellesley__ __Norfolk__ __02181__
        (Street and No.)   (City or Town)   (County)   (Zip)

Date of Death (4) __June 25, 1996__

Will and Death Certificate shall be filed with application.

Name and address of Applicant(s) (5) __Joan M. Williams__ __42 Newmarket Street__
__Wellesley, MA 02181__   Status (6) __Surviving Spouse/Named Executrix__

Your Applicant(s) respectfully state(s) that said estate consisting entirely of personal property the total value of which does not exceed fifteen thousand dollars ($15,000) exclusive of the decedent's automobile as shown by the following schedule of all the assets of said deceased known to the applicant(s):

Name of Property		Estimated Value
Bank Account - Bank of Boston - Acct. A33721	(7) $	2,880.00
US Savings Bond	$	1,000.00
1994 Honda Civic - VIN # A22098TT778	$	N/A
	$	
	$	
Total	$	3,880.00

That thirty days have expired since the date of death of said deceased and no petition for probate of will or appointment of administration/administratrix has been filed in said Court.

That your applicant(s) has __s__ undertaken to act as voluntary executor/executrix of the estate of said deceased and will administer the same according to law and apply the proceeds thereof in conformity with Section 16A of Chapter 195 of the General Laws.

That to the knowledge of the applicant(s) the following are the names and addresses of all persons surviving who, with the deceased, were joint owners of property; also listed are the names and addresses of those who would take under the provisions of Section 3 of Chapter 190 in the case of intestacy, and the names and addresses of those who would take under the provisions of the will.

(8)
Joan M. Williams	42 Newmarket Street, Wellesley, MA 02181
James T. Williams	2 Rock Road, Norfolk, Virginia
Mary K. Williams	15 Old Field Road, Lexington, MA 02173

(9) [X] The applicant(s) hereby certif __ies__ that a copy of this document, along with a copy of the decedent's death certificate has been sent by certified mail to the **Department of Public Welfare, P.O. Box 86, Essex Station, Boston, Massachusetts 02112.**

Date __7/5/96__   Signature __(10)__ _Joan M. Williams_
                                Joan M. Williams

(11) **NOTARIZATION**

_____ ss   Date _____

Then personally appeared __Joan M. Williams__
to me known and made oath that the information contained in the foregoing statement is true to the best of his/her/~~their~~ knowledge and belief.

Before me, _____
        NOTARY PUBLIC/JUSTICE OF THE PEACE

My Commission expires _____

CJ-P7A (8/92)

15

Petition for Voluntary Administration

Purpose: Petition for Voluntary Administration is utilized when the decedent's total assets do not exceed $15,000.00 excluding the value of any automobile, and the decedent did not have a valid last will and testament at the time of death.

1) County of decedent's residence at time of death.

2) Name of decedent.

3) Domicile at date of death.

4) Date of death.

5) Name and address of Petitioner.

6) Status, i.e. relationship and status as executor/executrix.

7) Listing of all assets and estimated value (not to exceed $15,000.00 in total).

8) Listing of all heirs at law and joint owners of property.

9) Copy of the Petition along with the death certificate must be mailed to the Department of Public Welfare.

10) Signature line for Petitioner.

11) The signature of the petitioner must be notarized, with the notary affixing his/her seal to the document.

Form 2

Commonwealth of Massachusetts
The Trial Court
Probate and Family Court Department

Docket No. _____

Voluntary Administration

(1) Norfolk Division

Name of Decedent (2) Steven J. Williams

Domicile at Death (3) 42 Newmarket Street   Wellesley   Norfolk   02181
(Street and No.)   (City or Town)   (County)   (Zip)

Date of Death (4) June 25, 1996

Death Certificate shall be filed with application.

Name and address of Applicant(s) (5) Joan M. Williams – 42 Newmarket St., Wellesley, MA 02181   Status (6) Surviving Spouse / Administratrix

Your applicant(s) respectfully state(s) that said estate consisting entirely of personal property the total value of which does not exceed fifteen thousand dollars ($15,000) exclusive of the decedent's automobile as shown by the following schedule of all the assets of said deceased known to the applicant(s):

Name of Property	Estimated Value
(7) Bank Account – Bank of Boston – Acct. No. A33721	$ 2,880.00
US Savings Bond	$ 1,000.00
1994 Honda Civic – VIN #A22098TT778	$ N/A
	$
	$
Total	$ 3,880.00

That thirty days have expired since the date of death of said deceased and no petition for probate of will or appointment of administration/administratrix has been filed in said Court.

That your applicant(s) ha__ undertaken to act as voluntary administrator/administratrix of the estate of said deceased and will administer the same according to law and apply the proceeds thereof in conformity with Section 16 of Chapter 195 of the General Laws.

That to the knowledge of the applicant(s) the following are the names and addresses of all persons surviving who, with the deceased, were joint owners of property; also listed are the names and addresses of those who would take under the provisions of Section 3 of Chapter 190 in the case of intestacy.

(8) Joan M. Williams   42 Newmarket Street, Wellesley, MA   02181
James T. Williams   2 Rock Road, Norfolk, Virginia
Mary K. Williams   15 Old Field Road, Lexington, MA   02173

(9) [X] The applicant(s) hereby certif ies that a copy of this document, along with a copy of the decedent's death certificate has been sent by certified mail to the **Department of Public Welfare, P.O. Box 86, Essex Station, Boston, Massachusetts 02112.**

Signature (10) Joan M. Williams
Joan M. Williams

(11) **NOTARIZATION**

Date 7/5/96

_____, ss.   Date _____, 19___

Then personally appeared Joan M. Williams to me known and made oath that the information contained in the foregoing statement is true to the best of his/her knowledge and belief.

Before me, _____ NOTARY PUBLIC/JUSTICE OF THE PEACE

My Commission expires _____

CJ-P7 (8/92)

Chapter 2
Probate of the Large Estate-With a Will

Probate When There is a Will

Under Massachusetts law, any person having the custody of a will must within 30 days of that person's receiving knowledge of the death of the creator of the will, deliver to the probate court the original will. The probate court for the county in which the decedent resided is the court in which the decedent's will must be probated. As a general proposition, the purpose of the probate court process is to be certain that a person's wishes as expressed in their will are fully honored.

Each county has a probate court which handles the probate of estates of decedents who resided in that county. The probate court has jurisdiction over a variety of matters including estates of decedents; trusts; guardianships; conservatorships; change of name; matters relating to the care, custody and education of minors; adoption; and divorce.

In Massachusetts, the assets which fall under the probate court's jurisdiction are most commonly those assets a person owns in their own name at the time of death. In such a case, the asset is "frozen" until the probate court can appoint an executor or administrator to take charge of the assets. Frozen assets can be cash, mutual funds, real estate, etc. Obtaining the decree of appointment as executor or administrator is often the most important step in the probate process to the decedent's survivors. Once appointed, an executor or administrator has full authority to deal with the decedent's assets. This will facilitate the payment of debts, taxes and the financial needs of a surviving spouse and family members. As will be pointed out several times in these materials it is extremely important to remember that only those assets in a person's name at the time of death fall within the probate court's jurisdiction.

Petition to Probate the Will

When a decedent dies having a valid will the probate process begins by having the executor prepare a Petition to Probate Will. The petition summarizes the information about the decedent as well as the decedent's heirs at law and next of kin. In the event an heir is a minor then it must be reflected on the petition.

If the Executor named in the will is unable to serve as executor, then he or she must decline to serve by way of a written declination. The successor executor named in the will would then petition to be named the Executor. If there was no successor named, then the process would be converted to an Administration with the will annexed.

The petition must be signed by the executor and if possible should be signed by all of the heirs. As will be true in almost all probate processes, the process is far easier when all interested parties assent (or approve) of the action being undertaken.

When completing the Petition to Probate Will care must be given to properly crossing out the unnecessary language or filling in the spaces provided. Since the probate court form is a standard form document it is necessary that it be tailored to each particular instance.

The petition also requires that a copy of the petition along with a copy of the decedent's death certificate be sent by *certified mail* to the Department of Public Welfare. The address for the Department of Public Welfare is PO Box 86, Essex Station, Boston, Massachusetts 02112. The purpose of this is to cross-reference the probate records with the records of the Department of Public Welfare to determine whether recipients of Medicaid benefits had assets that might be subject to recovery after death. Under present law, the Department of Public Welfare has the right to recover from the estate of a decedent funds which may have been spent during lifetime to provide for the decedent's care.

Purpose of Petition to Probate Will

As the starting point of the probate process the Petition serves two main functions. The first is to formally present the will for allowance by the court as the decedent's true last will and testament. Proving and allowing the will as the decedent's last will and testament requires that the court provide an opportunity to interested persons to raise any objection they may have to the validity of the document.

The second purpose of the Petition to Probate Will is to provide an opportunity for interested parties to object or otherwise express interest in the person petitioning to be named as executor. Again, the court process is one that is designed to allow interested people the opportunity to be heard prior to the appointment of the individual.

Filing the Petition

Once the Petition to Probate Will is prepared and signed by the executor and all necessary interested people, the petition should be filed with the probate court with the following documents:

1.	Original Last Will and Testament;
2.	Death Certificate;
3.	Bond;
4.	Payment of Filing Fees.

Last Will and Testament

Only the most recent, properly signed, original last will and testament should be filed with the probate court along with any codicils (amendments) to the will.

Death Certificate

A certified copy of the death certificate must be filed with the probate court to begin the process. Typically copies of the death certificate can be obtained from the funeral director or from the town clerk of the town in which the decedent died. Certified copies of the death certificate can also be obtained from the Registry of Vital Statistics located in Boston, Massachusetts. Care must be taken to review the information provided on the death certificate prior to beginning the preparation of the probate documents. Very often the death certificate will have a different date of death than the family members may have indicated to you. Unless there is obvious and gross error the information on the death certificate should be followed.

Bond

The probate bond is a guaranty signed by the Executor that he or she will properly perform the required duties in accordance with Massachusetts law. This is explained in more detail in Chapter 4.

Payment of Filing Fees

Presently the Petition to Probate Will incurs a fifty dollar filing fee. There is an additional ten dollar fee for opening a new docket.

The Citation

Once the above documents have been filed with the probate court the court will open a file (a docket) and assign a number to the case file. The probate court will then forward to the executor the necessary paperwork to begin notification of the Petition to Probate the Will. This notification is known as a citation. The citation is fully completed by the probate court and dictates to the type of notice that must be given. As with almost all probate court processes the court wants to ensure that every person who should be made aware of the probate process is given an opportunity to obtain that information. For this reason the court will specify which individuals are to receive specific notice of the probate process and will dictate where and in what newspaper a copy of the citation must be published.

Publishing the Citation

In reviewing the citation, the information which must be published is the information appearing above the words **Order of Notice**. The top two-thirds of this document provides information about the process, the person who was petitioning to be named executor, the date upon which you must file an objection if you wish to make one and the location of the probate court in which to make the objection.

To publish the citation you must contact the newspaper which is specified in the lower portion of this citation and obtain information as to when the legal notices are published and where this citation must be sent to be published. In most cases the notice is published in a local newspaper which is published only once per week. For this reason and because of the deadline established by the court in preparing the citation, it is necessary that you contact the newspaper immediately.

Never forward the original citation to a newspaper to be published as the original citation must be returned to the probate court. Losing or misplacing the original citation can cause great delay in the probate process.

When forwarding the citation to the newspaper for publication it is wise to ask that the newspaper fax to you a proof prior to publication so that you may review the actual legal notice prior to publication. This will provide you an opportunity to uncover any typographical mistakes. Once published you should request that the newspaper forward a tear sheet to you so that you will have a copy of the publication for your files.

Notices

The citation will also dictate the nature and form of notices which must be sent. The typical citation will require that all persons interested in the estate be provided a copy of the notice by delivering or mailing by postpaid a copy of the citation at least fourteen days before the return date. Common practice is to send these notices via certified mail so that there will be evidence of the receipt of the notice.

Return of Citation to Probate Court

On each citation appears a date upon which the interested parties must file a written objection and appearance in the probate court or be barred from raising those issues any further. This date is known as the return date. Once the return date has passed and all publication and delivery of notices has been made, the petitioner will return the original Order of Notice to the probate court. The bottom portion of the citation entitled, **RETURN OF SERVICE** needs to be completed by finishing the end of the sentence that has already been started as follows, "I hereby certify under the penalties of perjury that I have served the foregoing citation by *publishing and mailing as ordered*. This then needs to be signed by the Petitioner and dated and returned to the probate court. Returning to the probate court this citation is the evidence needed by the court to determine whether any objections have been made and if no objections have been made to appoint the executor.

Probate of Will

Purpose: This form is used when the decedent died having a will and the named executor or successor executor is willing and able to serve as executor.

1) Insert the county in which the decedent was domiciled at time of death.

2) Full name of decedent including any aliases.

3) Domicile at date of death

4) Date of Death

5) Name and address of person petitioning to be named executor

6) Insert status of person petitioning, meaning executor or successor executor.

7) List all heirs at law and next of kin providing the residential address and relationship to decedent.

8) A copy of the Petition and the death certificate must be mailed certified mail to the Department of Public Welfare.

9) The correct words need to be included and unnecessary words deleted to have the Petition read correctly.

10) The petitioner needs to sign the Petition. All heirs at law and next of kin should sign the Petition to facilitate filing.

11) Signatures of all heirs at law and next of kin.

Form 3

Commonwealth of Massachusetts
The Trial Court
Probate and Family Court Department

(1) Norfolk Division   Docket No. _____

Probate of Will With/Without Sureties

Name of Decedent (2) Steven J. Williams

Domicile at Death (3) 42 Newmarket Street, Wellesley Norfolk 02181
(Street and No.) (City or Town) (County) (Zip)

Date of Death (4) June 25, 1996

Name and address of Petitioner(s) (5) Joan M. Williams
42 Newmarket Street, Wellesley, MA 02181
Status (6) Surviving Spouse/Named Executor

Heirs at law or next of kin of deceased including surviving spouse
(minors and incompetents must be so designated)

Name	Residence	Relationship
Joan M. Williams	42 Newmarket Street, Wellesley, MA 02181	Surviving Spouse
James T. Williams	2 Rock Road, Norfolk VA	Son
Mary E. Williams	15 Old Field Road, Lexington, MA 02173	Daughter

That said deceased left a will — and codicils — herewith presented, wherein your petitioner(s) is/are named execut rix and wherein the testator had requested that your petitioner(s) be exempt from giving surety on his/her/their bond(s).

(8) [X] The petitioner(s) hereby certif ies that a copy of this document, along with a copy of the decedent's death certificate has been sent by certified mail to the **Department of Public Welfare. P.O. Box 86. Essex Station. Boston, Massachusetts 02112.**

(9) Wherefore your petitioner(s) pray(s) that said will — and codicils — may be proved and allowed, and that he/she/they be appointed execut rix thereof, with/without surety on his/her/their bond(s) and certif ies under the penalties of perjury that the statements herein contained are true to the best of his/her/their knowledge and belief.

Date 7/15/96   Signature(s) (10) Joan M. Williams

Joan M. Williams

DECREE

The undersigned hereby assent to the foregoing petition and to the allowance of the will without testimony.

Dave T. Williams
James T. Williams

(11) _Joan M. Williams_
Joan M. Williams
Mary E. Williams
Mary E. Williams

All persons interested having been notified in accordance with the law or having assented and no objections being made thereto, it is decreed that said instrument(s) be approved and allowed as the last will and testament of said deceased, and that said petitioner(s):
of _____
and _____ be appointed
execut _____ thereof, first giving bond with _____ sureties for the due performance of said trust.

Date _____

_____
JUSTICE OF THE PROBATE AND FAMILY COURT

CJ-P2 (8/92)

Declination

Purpose: The Declination is used when the named executor in a will is unable or unwilling to act as executor.

1) Name of person named in the will who does not wish to serve.

2) Name of decedent.

3) Signature line for person declining the position.

COMMONWEALTH OF MASSACHUSETTS.
THE TRIAL COURT

To the Honorable the Justices of the Probate and Family Court, in and for the County of Norfolk:

It being inconvenient for . . (1) . Joan M. Williams . . . .

to discharge the duty of execut rix ~~afxxxxxxxx~~ under – the last will and testament of

. (2) . Steven J. Williams . . . .

late of . . Wellesley . . . . .in said County of . . Norfolk . . . . . ",

deceased, ... do hereby decline that trust.

Dated this . . . . . 15th . . . . .day of . . . . July 19 96

(3). *Joan M. Williams*
Joan M. Williams

General Assent

Purpose: The General Assent is a document used to obtain signatures from interested parties approving of a particular action or petition of an estate fiduciary. The General Assent form is used to obtain signatures of interested parties so that the original Petition need not be forwarded to each individual.

1) County of decedent's residence at the time of death.

2) Name of the estate.

3) Reference to the particular matter for which approval is sought.

4) The name of the heir or next of kin interested in the estate to whom this is addressed.

5) Signature line for the interested party.

Form 5

Commonwealth of Massachusetts
The Trial Court
Probate and Family Court Department

Docket No. _____

(1) __Norfolk__ Division

General Assent

Estate of (2) __Steven J. Williams__ _____

In the matter of (3) __the Petition to Probate Will__ _____

(4) I, __John T. Williams__ _____ of __Dedham, Massachusetts__ _____

being a party interested in the above matter hereby consent to the allowance of the same by the Probate and Family Court for this County and request that the same be granted without further notice.

_____ _____ (5) _John T. Williams_
Witness   Date   Signature

Release Of All Demands And Assent To Account

In the matter of _____

In consideration of _____

paid by _____ , the receipt whereof is hereby acknowledged

I, _____ of _____

do hereby release and forever discharge the said _____

from all debts and liabilities whatsoever which I now have for or on account of the estate of _____

_____

and I further consent to the allowance of the petition — account — appointment described above.

_____ _____ _____
Witness   Date   Signature

CJ-P 21 (8/86)

23

Appointment of Agent

Purpose:

When an estate fiduciary does not reside in the Commonwealth of Massachusetts it is necessary that a resident of the Commonwealth of Massachusetts be appointed for purpose of having any process served on a representative.

1) County of decedent's residence at the time of death.

2) Name of agent not residing in Massachusetts.

3) Name of Massachusetts resident to whom service may be made.

4) Name of estate and address of decedent at time of death.

5) Signature of the out-of-state estate fiduciary.

6) The acceptance of the Massachusetts resident of the appointment.

Form 6

Commonwealth of Massachusetts
The Trial Court
Probate and Family Court Department

Docket No. _____

(1) Norfolk _____ Division

Appointment of Agent

I, (2) James T. Williams _____ of _2 Rock Road_ _____
(Street and No.)

Richmond _____ Virginia _____ appoint
(City or Town) (County) (State) (Zip)

(3) Joan M. Williams _____ of

42 Newmarket Street, Wellesley, _____ Norfolk _____ 02181
(Street and No.) (City or Town) (County) (Zip)

as my agent and I do stipulate and agree that the service of any legal process against me as administrator/administratrix —executor/~~executrix/trustee~~ — of the estate of (4) Steven J. Williams

late of _42 Newmarket Street_ _____
(Street and No.)

Wellesley _____ Norfolk _____ 02181
(City or Town) (County) (Zip)

or as guardian/conservator of _____

of _____ _____
(Street and No.) (City or Town) (County) (Zip)

or against me in my individual capacity of any action founded upon or arising out of my acts or omissions as such fiduciary if made on said agent, shall have like effect as if made on me personally within said Commonwealth.

Signature (5) _James T. Williams_

Date _____

Signed in the presence of _____ _____
WITNESS

Acceptance

I, (6) Joan M. Williams _____ accept the above appointment.

42 Newmarket Street _____ Wellesley _____ MA _____ 02181
(Street and No.) (City or Town) (State) (Zip)

CJ-P17 (4/89)

Military Affidavit

Purpose: The Military Affidavit must be filed in all cases in which all assents of heirs at law and interested people have not been obtained. This Affidavit provides information about the military status of any heir at law or interested party.

1) County of decedent's residence at the time of death.

2) Name of estate.

3) Address of decedent.

4) Date of death.

5) The subject matter to which this relates.

6) The estate fiduciary's name and address.

7) Cross out the necessary language to accurately reflect the military status of any of the interested persons or heirs at law.

8) Signature of estate fiduciary.

Form 7

Commonwealth of Massachusetts
The Trial Court
Probate and Family Court Department

(1) Norfolk _____ **Division**   Docket No. _____

Military Affidavit

Estate of _____ (2) Steven J. Williams

late of (3) 42 Newmarket Street _____ Wellesley
(street and no.)   (city or town)

Norfolk _____ 02181 _____ Date of Death (4) June 25, 1996
(county)   (zip)

In the matter of the — petition — ~~XXXXXXXX~~ of (5) Joan M. Williams

~~XXXXXXXX~~ _____

_____

I, (6) Joan M. Williams _____ of _____ 42 Market Street,
                                          (street and no.)

Wellesley, _____ Norfolk _____ 02181
(city or town)   (county)   (zip)

on oath depose and say that none of the — heirs-at-law — parties interested — in said petition — ~~complaint~~ — ~~account~~ — are in the military service of the United States or citizens of the United States in the military service of its allies.

on oath depose and say that _____

on oath depose and say that I am unable to determine whether or not

heirs-at-law — parties interested — in said petition — complaint — account — are in the military service of the United States or citizens of the United States in the military service of its allies.

heirs-at-law — parties interested — in said petition — complaint — account — are in the military service of the United States or citizens of the United States in the military service of its allies.

Signed under the penalties of perjury this _____ day of _____ 19 ____

Signature (8) _Joan M. Williams_
              Joan M. Williams

CJ-P 148 (1/89)

Chapter 3
Probate of a Large Estate - Without a Will

In instances where a person passes away not having a valid will in place, the person is known as having died intestate. In such a case Massachusetts law provides a distribution scheme so that the assets of the decedent may pass to his heirs and next of kin.

The most common distribution scheme provides that if the decedent left a surviving spouse and issue (children) then the surviving spouse would take one-half of the real property and the issue take the balance. If the decedent left a surviving spouse, but no issue, but did leave kindred (blood relatives of the decedent) then the surviving spouse would take $200,000.00 and one-half of the remaining real property and the kindred would take the balance. If the decedent left no issue and no kindred then the surviving spouse would inherit everything.

Once it is determined who the heirs and kindred are that will inherit from the decedent, the Petition to Probate can be completed. In cases where there is no valid will the form of probate is known as an Administration.

The Petition to commence an administration is very similar to the Petition to Probate Will and requests the same information from the Petitioner.

Who May Serve as Administrator?

Massachusetts law provides an order of preference for the person who may serve as administrator. The first such person is the surviving spouse. If the surviving spouse cannot or will not serve then the next of kin can serve as administrator. Absent spouse or next of kin then the Petition for Administration can be commenced by a creditor seeking the recover funds due from the estate. In the absence of any of these individuals then the administration can be commenced by a public administrator. The public administrator is a person named by the governor to serve in a particular county to undertake administrations when there is no spouse or living heirs in the commonwealth who can be appointed Administrator. The public Administrator's role is to marshal the assets and expenses of the estate, settle all estate matters and distribute the assets to the heirs. If there are no heirs to be located then the assets will be turned over to the state treasurer.

Filing the Petition

Once the Petition for Administration is prepared and signed by the Administrator and all necessary interested people, the petition should be filed with the probate court with the following documents:

1. Death Certificate;
2. Bond;
3. Payment of Filing Fees.

Death Certificate

A certified copy of the death certificate must be filed with the probate court to begin the process. Typically copies of the death certificate can be obtained from the funeral director or from the town clerk of the town in which the decedent died. Certified copies of the death certificate can also be obtained from the Registry of Vital Statistics located in Boston, Massachusetts. Care must be taken to review the information provided on the death certificate prior to beginning the preparation of the probate documents. Very often the death certificate will have a different date of death than the family members may have indicated to you. Unless there is obvious and gross error the information on the death certificate should be followed.

Bond

The probate bond is a guaranty signed by the Administrator that he or she will properly perform the required duties in accordance with Massachusetts law. This is explained in detail in Chapter 4.

Payment of Filing Fees

Presently the petition for administration incurs a fifty dollar filing fee. There is an additional ten dollar fee for opening a new docket.

The Citation

Once the above documents have been filed with the probate court the court will open a file (a docket) and assign a number to the case file. The probate court will then forward to the administrator the necessary paperwork to begin notification of the Administration. This notification is known as a citation. The citation is fully completed by the probate court and dictates to the type of notice that must be given. As will almost all probate court processes the court wants to ensure that every person who should be made aware of the probate process is given an opportunity to obtain that information. For this reason the court will specify which individuals are to receive specific notice of the probate process and will dictate where and in what newspaper a copy of the citation must be published.

Publishing the Citation

In reviewing the citation, the information which must be published is the information appearing above the words **Order of Notice**. The top two-thirds of this document provides information about the process, the person who was petitioning to be named executor, the date upon which you must file an objection if you wish to make one and the location of the probate court in which to make the objection.

To publish the citation you must contact the newspaper which is specified in the lower portion of this citation and obtain information as to when the legal notices are published and where this citation must be sent to be published. In most cases the notice is published in a local newspaper which is published only once per week. For this reason and because of the deadline established by the court in preparing the citation, it is necessary that you contact the newspaper immediately.

Never forward the original citation to a newspaper to be published as the original citation must be returned to the probate court. Losing or misplacing the original citation can cause great delay in the probate process.

When forwarding the citation to the newspaper for publication it is wise to ask that the newspaper fax to you a proof prior to publication so that you may review the actual legal notice prior to publication. This will provide you an opportunity to uncover any typographical mistakes. Once published you should request that the newspaper forward a tear sheet to you so that you will have a copy of the publication for your files.

Notices

The citation will also dictate the nature and form of notices which must be sent. The typical citation will require that all persons interested in the estate be provided a copy of the notice by delivering or mailing by postpaid a copy of the citation at least fourteen days before the return date. Common practice is to send these notices via certified mail so that there will be evidence of the receipt of the notice.

Return of Citation to Probate Court

On each citation appears a date upon which the interested parties must file a written objection and appearance in the probate court or be barred from raising those issues any further. This date is known as the return date. Once the return date has passed and all publication and delivery of notices has been made, the petitioner will return the original Order of Notice to the probate court. The bottom portion of the citation entitled, **RETURN OF SERVICE** needs to be completed by finishing the end of the sentence that has been started as follows, "I hereby certify under the penalties of perjury that I have served the foregoing citation by *publishing and mailing as ordered*. This then needs to be signed by the Petitioner and dated and returned to the probate court. Returning to the probate court this citation is the evidence needed by the court to determine whether any objections have been made and if no objections have been made to appoint the Administrator.

Administration

Purpose: An administration is used when the decedent died without a valid will and testament (intestate).

1) Insert the county in which the decedent was domiciled at time of death.

2) Full name of decedent including any aliases.

3) Domicile at date of death

4) Date of Death

5) Name and address of person petitioning to be named executor

6) Insert status of person petitioning, meaning executor or successor executor

7) List all heirs at law and next of kin providing the residential address and relationship to decedent

8) A copy of the Petition and the death certificate must be mailed certified mail to the Department of Public Welfare

9) The correct words need to be included and unnecessary words deleted to have the Petition read correctly.

10) The petitioner needs to sign the Petition.

11) All heirs at law and next of kin should sign the Petition to facilitate filing.

Form 8

Commonwealth of Massachusetts
The Trial Court
Probate and Family Court Department   Docket No. _____

(1) ___Norfolk___ Division

Administration With/Without Sureties

Name of Decedent (2) __Steven J. Williams__

Domicile at Death (3) __42 Newmarket Street__ __Wellesley__ __Norfolk__ __02181__
            (Street and No.)   (City or Town)   (County) (Zip)

Date of Death (4) __June 25, 1996__

Name and address of Petitioner(s) (5) __Joan M. Williams__
__42 Newmarket Street, Wellesley, MA 02181__
Status (6) __Surviving Spouse__

Heirs at law or next of kin of deceased including surviving spouse:

(7)

Name	Residence (minors and incompetents must be so designated)	Relationship
Joan M. Williams	42 Newmarket Street, Wellesley, MA 02181	Surviving Spouse
James T. Williams	2 Rock Road, Norfolk, VA	Son
Mary E. Williams	15 Old Field Road, Lexington, MA 02173	Daughter

(8) ☒ The petitioner(s) hereby certif __Y__ that a copy of the decedent's death certificate has been sent by certified mail to the **Department of Public Welfare, P.O. Box 86, Essex Station, Boston, Massachusetts 02112.**

(9) Petitioner(s) pray(s) that he/she/they or some other suitable person _____ be appointed administrator of _____ in the County of _____ of said estate with/without surety on his/her/their bond(s) and certif __ies__ under the penalties of perjury that the foregoing statements are true to the best of his/her/their knowledge and belief.

Signature(s) (10) _Joan M. Williams_
Joan M. Williams

Date _____

The undersigned hereby assent to the foregoing petition.

(11) _Joan M. Williams_   _James T. Will_
Joan M. Williams   James T. Williams

Mary K. Williams
Mary K. Williams

DECREE

All persons interested having been notified in accordance with the law or having assented and no objections being made thereto, it is decreed that _____ be appointed administrat _____ of said estate first giving bond of _____ in the County of _____ with _____ sureties for the due performance of said trust.

Date _____   _____
                    JUSTICE OF THE PROBATE AND FAMILY COURT

CJ-P1 (8/92)

Probate of Will - Administration with the Will Annexed

Purpose: This form is used when there is a valid will but the named executor and successor executor are no longer living or capable of serving.

1) Insert the county in which the decedent was domiciled at time of death.

2) Full name of decedent including any aliases.

3) Domicile at date of death

4) Date of Death

5) Name and address of person petitioning to be named executor

6) Insert status of person petitioning, meaning executor or successor executor

7) List all heirs at law and next of kin providing the residential address and relationship to decedent

8) A copy of the Petition and the death certificate must be mailed certified mail to the Department of Public Welfare

9) The correct words need to be included and unnecessary words deleted to have the Petition read correctly.

10) The petitioner needs to sign the Petition.

11) All heirs at law and next of kin should sign the Petition to facilitate filing.

Form 9

Commonwealth of Massachusetts
The Trial Court
(1) __Norfolk__ Division   Probate and Family Court Department   Docket No. _____

Probate Of Will - Administration With The Will Annexed
~~With~~ - Without - Sureties

Name of Decedent (2) __Steven J. Williams__

Domicile at Death (3) __42 Newmarket Street__ __Wellesley__
(street and no.)   (city or town)

__Norfolk__   __02181__ Date of Death (4) __June 25, 1996__
(county)   (zip)

Name and address of Petitioner(s) (5) __Mary K. Williams, 15 Old Field Road, Lexington,__

__Massachusetts 02173__   Status (6) __Daughter__

Heirs at law or next of kin of deceased including surviving spouse:

Name	Residence	Relationship
(7)	(minors and incompetents must be so designated)	
Joan M. Williams	42 Newmarket Street, Wellesley, MA 02181	Surviving Spous
James T. Williams	2 Rock Road, Norfolk, Virginia	Son
Mary K. Williams	15 Old Field Road, Lexington, MA 02173	Daughter

That said deceased left a will ~~and codicils~~ — herewith presented, wherein __Joan M. Williams__

serve — ~~and codicils herewith presented~~ is named ~~executor/~~ executrix but has — declined to

(8) [X] The petitioner(s) hereby certif__ies__ that a copy of this document, along with a copy of the decedent's death certificate has been sent by certified mail to the **Department of Public Welfare, P.O. Box 86, Essex Station, Boston, Massachusetts 02112.**

(9) Wherefore your petitioner(s) pray(s) that said will ~~and codicil(s)~~ — may be proved and allowed, and that he/she/they or some other suitable person _____

of _____ _____ _____
(street and no.)   (city or town)   (county)   (zip)

be appointed administrator/administratrix with the will annexed, — ~~with~~ — without — sureties on ~~his/~~her bond, and certif__ies__ under the penalties of perjury that the statements herein contained are true to the best of ~~his/~~her/ ~~his~~ knowledge and belief.

Date _____   Signature (10) _Mary K Williams_
    Mary K. Williams
    James T. Williams
    James T. Williams

The undersigned hereby assent to the foregoing petition and to the allowance of the will without testimony.

(11) _Joan M. Williams_
    Joan M. Williams
    Mary K. Williams
    Mary K. Williams

DECREE

All persons interested having been notified in accordance with the law or having assented and no objections being made thereto, it is decreed that said instrument(s) be approved and allowed as the last will and testament of said deceased, and that _____ in the County of _____

be appointed administrat____ with the will annexed of said estate first giving bond, with _____ sureties, for the due performance of said trust.

Date _____   _____
    Justice of the Probate and Family Court

CJ-P 3 (8/92)

Special Administration

Purpose: The special administration is used when the appointment of an executor or administrator is delayed due to circumstances beyond anyone's control and assets of the estate require immediate attention.

1) County of decedent's residence.

2) Name of decedent with all aliases.

3) Address of decedent.

4) Date of death of decedent.

5) Name and address of Petitioner.

6) Status of Petitioner.

7) Include the necessary language to explain why a Special Administrator is necessary.

8) A copy of the Petition along with a copy of the death certificate needs to be sent certified mail to the Department of Public Welfare.

9) Signature line for the petitioner.

10) Signature lines for heirs at law and next of kin.

Form 10

Commonwealth of Massachusetts
The Trial Court

(1) Norfolk Division   Probate and Family Court Department   Docket No. ____

Special Administration

Name of Decedent (2) Steven J. Williams

Domicile at Death (3) 42 Newmarket Street,   Wellesley
            (street and no.)   (city or town)

Norfolk   02181   Date of Death (4) June 25, 1996
(county)   (zip)

Name and address of Petitioner(s) (5) Joane M. Williams, 42 Newmarket Street,

Wellesley, MA 02181   Status (6) Surviving Spouse

(7) Respectfully represent(s) that said decedent died possessed of goods and estate remaining to be administered, and that there is delay in securing the appointment of the Executor of the estate of said decedent by reason of the inability to obtain all necessary assets

(8) [X] The petitioner(s) hereby certifies that a copy of this document, along with a copy of the decedent's death certificate has been sent by certified mail to the **Department of Public Welfare, P.O. Box 86, Essex Station, Boston, Massachusetts 02112.**

Wherefore your petitioner(s) pray(s) that ~~he/she/they~~ or some other suitable person:

_____
(street and no.)

_____ may be appointed special
(city or town)   (county)   (zip)

~~administrator~~/administratrix of said decedent and may be authorized to take charge of all the real estate of said decedent and to collect rents and make necessary repairs; and may be authorized to continue the business of the decedent for the benefit of his/her estate, and certifies under the penalties of perjury that the statements herein contained are true to the best of his/her/their knowledge and belief.

Date _____ Signature (9) _Joan M. Williams_
                                         Joan M. Williams

The undersigned hereby assent to the foregoing petition.

(10) _Joan M. Williams_
Joan M. Williams

Mary K. Williams
Mary K. Williams

DECREE

All persons interested having been notified in accordance with the law or having assented and no objections being made thereto, it is decreed that _____ of _____

_____ in the County of _____ be appointed

administrat____ of said estate, first giving bond with _____ sureties, for the due performance of said trust.

Date _____ _____
                                            Justice of the Probate and Family Court

CJ-P 8 (8/92)

Chapter 4
The Probate Bond

The Probate Bond, which must be filed when any petition to be appointed in a fiduciary capacity is filed, is a written guarantee by the person requesting appointment that they will faithfully and properly perform the duties of the position consistent with the laws of the Commonwealth of Massachusetts. There are two types of probate bonds:

Bond with Sureties

A Bond with Sureties is a bond signed by the petitioner, being co-signed by an individual or an insurance company guaranteeing the petitioner's promise as stipulated in the bond. If two individuals are willing to sign the bond as guarantors then the bond can be filed with personal sureties. When completing a Bond with Personal Sureties the bond must show both the real estate value, the personal estate (non-real estate assets) and must contain a penal sum. The penal sum is calculated as an amount equal to one and one-half times the personal estate.

If an insurance company is to be the guarantor of the fiduciary's obligations, then the insurance company countersigns the bond but in such a case no penal sum is required. When a corporate surety is used, the insurance company charges an annual premium which must be paid until such time as the probate court Final Account is filed and allowed.

To obtain a corporate surety an insurance company will review the Executor/ Administrator's personal financial statement to determine whether the person is a good credit risk. The local property and casualty insurer can often help process a probate court bond. The cost of the corporate bond can approach $2,000 annually for a $1,000,000 bond.

Bonds without Sureties

A Bond without Sureties is a probate court bond that is signed only by the person petitioning to be named as the estate fiduciary. This is often the preferable form of bond to use as it does not require the fiduciary to obtain two other individuals to sign guaranteeing the obligations nor does it incur the expense of an insurance company for a corporate surety.

If the decedent in his will provides that the executor does not need to post sureties on his bond, then in most cases the court will allow the fiduciary to be appointed without sureties on the bond.

If the will does not specifically stipulate that no sureties are required then it will be necessary for all heirs at law and next of kin to approve of the executor serving without sureties for the court to allow it.

At the present time the filing fee for a bond is $30.00.

Bond

Purpose: The written guaranty to the probate court that the individual requesting to be named as the fiduciary will faithfully undertake the duties in accordance with Massachusetts law. This bond must be filed in every probate action in which the fiduciary will be appointed.

1) Insert the county in which the decedent was domiciled at time of death.

2) Type of fiduciary requesting appointment (executor, executrix, administrator, administratrix).

3) Indicate whether the bond is without surety, with personal surety or with corporate surety.

4) Name of decedent with all aliases included.

5) Name of petitioner with address.

6) Estimate of real estate subject to probate.

7) Estimate of personal estate subject to probate.

8) Penal sum - in cases with personal surety the penal sum is 1.5 times the estimated personal estate.

9) Complete the preprinted language to read properly.

10) The petitioner signs the bond.

11) If this is a bond with personal surety then the names and addresses of the two individuals signing as personal sureties must be included along with their signatures.

12) When filing a bond with personal sureties an attorney must sign indicating that the personal sureties are sufficient.

13) When a corporate surety is being issued the insurance company will complete this section.

Form 11

Commonwealth of Massachusetts
The Trial Court

(1) Norfolk **Division**   Probate and Family Court Department   Docket No. _____

(3)   (x) **without**
      (   ) **with Personal Surety**
      (   ) **with Corporate Surety**

Bond of (2) Executor
(type of fiduciary)

Name of Estate (4) Steven J. Williams

Name and Address of Fiduciary (5) Joan M. Williams, 42 Newmarket Street, Wellesley, MA 02181

Estimated Real Estate (6) $200,000.00   Estimated Personal Estate (7) $100,000.00

Penal Sum of Bond, (if applicable) (8) N/A

(9) I, **We**, the undersigned fiduciary accept appointment as _____Executrix_____ and stand bound ~~to the aforesaid penal sum~~ with the undersigned surety or sureties — (if applicable) to perform the statutory conditions of said bond and declare the above estimate to be to my ~~our~~ best knowledge and belief.

Date _____   (10) _Joan M. Williams_   Joan M. Will
                    Signature of Fiduciary — Principal

(complete below only if this is a bond with personal sureties)

We, the undersigned, as sureties, stand bound jointly and severally in the aforesaid penal sum to perform the statutory condition.

Personal Surety's Name and Address   (11) _____

_____ Signature

Personal Surety's Name and Address _____

_____ Signature

(12) The above sureties are in my opinion sufficient.

_____   by _____
Signature   Office   City or Town

(complete below only if this is a Surety Company Bond)

(13) We, the undersigned surety company, a corporation duly organized by law under the state of _____ and having a usual place of business in _____
(Massachusetts address)

stand bound as surety, in the aforesaid penal sum, to perform the statutory condition.

_____   by _____
Corporate Surety (name)   Signature and Title

_____ , ss. _____ 19____ examined and approved.

Justice ~~Assistant Register~~ of The Probate and Family Court

CJ-P 26 (1/89)

Chapter 5
The Inventory

The probate court Inventory is designed to obtain date of death asset information about the decedent and is prepared in blank by the probate court and forwarded to the executor once he or she has been appointed. Massachusetts law requires that every executor and administrator file the Inventory within three months of his or her appointment. There is no filing fee to be paid upon filing the Inventory. There is no late penalty for filing the Inventory after the three month period, however, the executor may be subject to an order by the court requiring the filing of the Inventory if an interested party so requests.

Preparing the Inventory

Every Inventory contains two sections, real estate and personal estate.

Real Estate

The Inventory will list all real estate owned by the decedent in the decedent's name alone or owned by the decedent as a tenant in common. The real estate should be described both by the address as well as by the appropriate book and page reference at the Registry of Deeds. The Inventory should list the appraised value of the property along with any outstanding mortgage owed on the property. This will provide the probate court with specific information about the equity value in the real estate.

Personal Estate

The Personal Estate of a decedent is everything other than real estate. Categories to be listed, in addition to others, are as follows:

Bank Accounts and Investments

Bank accounts, investments, promissory notes, mortgages, etc. must all be listed at their date of death value. All such assets should include accrued interest through date of death in valuing the assets. Each asset should be listed separately providing a separate date of death value.

Publicly Traded Stocks and Bonds

Publicly traded stocks and bonds must be listed at their date of death value. To be consistent with estate tax law the stocks and bonds should be valued using the same approach used by the IRS. Specifically, the stocks and bonds must be valued using the average of the high and low prices on the date of death. In cases where the date of death falls on a Saturday, Sunday or legal holiday, the value of the security or bond is obtained by taking the average of the prices on the days immediately before and after the weekend or holiday. As an example, a person passing away on Sunday would have their assets valued by taking the average of the high and low of the security on Friday and the average of the high and low of the security on Monday and then taking the average of the average.

Closely Held Stock

Valuation of closely held, non-publicly traded stock is extremely difficult. In instances where a large portion of a decedent's estate is comprised of closely held stock it may be necessary to hire a professional appraiser to establish the value of the decedent's interest in the enterprise.

Other Assets

Other assets such as personal property, jewelry, life insurance, patent rights, etc. should all be listed as assets owned by the decedent on the Inventory.

Items not Included

Since the probate court has jurisdiction over only those assets in the decedent's name alone, assets which were jointly held would not be included. In addition the following assets should not be listed on an Inventory:

1.   Payable on Death Accounts and jointly owned assets.

2.   Life insurance policies, Individual Retirement Accounts, Pension Plans, etc. in which there is a valid beneficiary designation naming somebody or some entity other than the decedent's estate.

3.   Assets in a trust which trust was created during the lifetime of the decedent.

4.   Automobiles that were owned by the decedent in his or her name alone that is going to pass to the surviving spouse.

Chapter 6
What to Do Once You are Appointed

Collecting Assets and Expenses

Since the role of the estate fiduciary is to administer the assets and liabilities of a decedent, it is important to gather all information necessary to properly undertake this job. To do this requires that a review be made of all of the decedent's personal effects and papers in an attempt to gather all outstanding liabilities and gain as much information as possible about assets that may be owned. A search should be made for prior years tax returns, bank statements, passbook accounts, mutual fund statements and information about safe deposit boxes. It is often suggested that the decedent's cancelled checks for the last year be reviewed to gain information about the monthly deposits being made and checks being written so that the estate representative can anticipate certain recurring expenses.

When possible, arrangements should be made with the post office so that all of the decedent's mail will be forwarded to the estate representative. The stream of mail will begin to dwindle as each institution, creditor and holder of asset is notified of the decedent's death. By having the mail forwarded to the estate representative, unknown assets and liabilities can be discovered some number of months after the decedent's death. To have the mail forwarded by the post office requires that the estate representative file a written request with the postmaster of the decedent's town along with a copy of the Certificate of Appointment as issued by the probate court and a copy of the decedent's death certificate.

Closing Accounts and Collecting Assets

Once the nature of the decedent's assets have been determined, the estate representative can begin the process of closing accounts and liquidating the assets.

Bank Accounts

To close bank accounts requires that contact be made with each bank in which the decedent maintained an account to obtain information about the documents that the bank will require to close the account. You should also obtain the address at which they would like all information sent since most banking institutions now have central locations for such work. This will avoid long delays when such paperwork is sent to the local branch and not the central banking registry. In most instances the bank will require the following:

1.   Letter of instructions signed by the Executor of Administrator.

2.   Copy of the decedent's death certificate.

3.   Original Certificate of Appointment as prepared by the probate court dated within sixty days of the date the letter is being sent to the bank.

Closing Stock Brokerage Accounts

Closing a stock brokerage account will require very similar formalities. Very often a stock brokerage house will require that an Affidavit of Domicile be prepared and filed with the other necessary paperwork. An Affidavit of Domicile is an affidavit signed by the Executor indicating the length of time that the decedent resided in the Commonwealth of Massachusetts and attesting to the fact that there are sufficient assets in the estate to pay all necessary liabilities and taxes.

What are the Rules for Paying Bills?

Shortly after appointment the estate representative should make a thorough and complete list of all outstanding debts owed by the decedent. A letter should be sent to each of these creditors notifying them of the decedent's death. When contacting credit card companies it is important to notify them that the account should be closed. In many cases the credit card company will require that the original credit card be returned to them. As a general rule the decedent's debts should not be paid until such time as it has been determined that there are sufficient assets to satisfy all of the "priority expenses."

Priority Expenses of an estate are the costs of the administration of the estate (executor fees, court fees, attorneys fees, etc.) taxes, funeral expenses and expenses of last illness. To be certain that the executor or administrator does not utilize all of the estate assets on expenses that are not "priority expenses" thereby exposing the fiduciary to personal liability, careful study of all expenses should be made to determine which expenses should be paid and when. A typical expense that might be paid during the early stages of a probate process would be utility bills for any real estate which the decedent owned in his or her name alone. In such a case it would be appropriate to contact the particular utility to discuss the possibility of deferring payments for some number of months. If an arrangement cannot be made with the utility then it would be important to utilize estate assets to pay these bills (electric, gas, oil) to preserve and protect the asset of the estate.

Do I Need an Identification Number for the Estate / How do I get one?

If the decedent owned assets which require a formal probate administration then in almost all cases it will be necessary to obtain a Federal Identification Number. It is impossible to open a bank account or a checking account in the name of the estate unless you have a federal identification number. To obtain such a number requires the completion of IRS Form SS4, Application for Identification Number. Once completed and signed by the Executor/Administrator the application should be filed with the Internal Revenue Service at the Andover Service Center. The address is: Internal Revenue Service, Andover Service Center, Andover, Massachusetts 05501. The Application can also be filed by faxing it to the IRS - Tel Tin at (508) 474- 9758. If requested in the fax cover sheet, the IRS will call the estate representative and provide him/her the identification number over the telephone. This will save up to three weeks of time waiting for a written response from the IRS.

What Should You Do with Estate Assets?

Once the bank accounts, etc. have been closed the estate fiduciary has an obligation to properly invest and manage the estate assets. Since most probate matters and the assets being administered are closed and distributed within 12 to 14 months of the decedent's death the estate fiduciary will want to invest the estate assets in liquid investments that have very little risk. The executor has a duty to make the assets productive, however, the executor also has an obligation to administer the assets as a reasonably prudent person would do. Given the short period of time that an executor or administrator will have possession of the estate assets it would not seem prudent to invest the assets in speculative investments.

If at the time of the decedent's death the decedent owned large amounts of publicly traded securities a careful review of these securities should be made by the legal representative. Concern must be given to any particular security which is heavily weighted in the decedent's portfolio as a downturn in that particular security could cause substantial reduction in the value of the estate assets. The executor of administrator's obligation is to be certain that the investments of the estate assets is safe and secure for the benefit of the beneficiaries. An investment strategy undertaken by a decedent prior to death is not always consistent with the obligations and investment strategies of an executor or administrator. In these cases it is often wise to obtain the assistance of an investment professional to analyze the portfolio and make suggestions to minimize the investment risk to the estate.

What Shouldn't You Do with Estate Assets?

The obligation of the executor, and the understanding when filing the probate bond, is that the executor or administrator will faithfully and properly administer the probate estate. As such, the executor or administrator is personally liable for actions which are not done in accordance with law or are not reasonable given the standard of care that must be maintained. For example, a legal representative who invests the estate assets in speculative or risky investments and loses the assets could be liable for his or her poor judgment. As a general rule you should never do any of the following:

1.   Leverage or margin the estate assets.

2.   Borrow the estate assets.

3.   Use estate assets to pay bills or expenses of the executor or administrator.

4.   Invest the assets in speculative or risky investments.

5.   Lend assets of the estate unless the interested parties, heirs, etc. all approve of the transaction in writing.

Insurance Benefits

When locating insurance policies in the course of reviewing the decedent's personal effects, the policies should be reviewed to determine who the proper beneficiary is. If the policy does not provide that information then only the legal representative of the estate and the specific beneficiary may contact the insurance company for additional information. The executor or administrator should contact the insurance company to provide them notice of the decedent's death and to inquire as to the nature of the benefits and the name of the beneficiary. If the designated beneficiary is the "Estate of the Decedent" then executor or administrator would receive the insurance proceeds and add that to the assets being managed in the probate estate. If the beneficiary designation is an individual who is living then, the executor or administrator would need to provide that person information about the insurance policy. No other action would need to be taken by the executor or administrator as the insurance benefits would not be part of the probate estate.

Social Security Benefits

Federal law dictates that a recipient of social security benefits must survive the entire month to retain the benefits paid on the first day of the month. In the ordinary course the benefits are mailed or direct-deposited in the first two or three days of the calendar month. If a person passes away before the end of the month then the entire social security check must be returned to the Social Security Administration. This should be done as soon as possible to prevent the Social Security Administration from continuing to send monthly checks after the decedent's death.

AFFIDAVIT OF DOMICILE

Commonwealth of Massachusetts

Norfolk , ss.   July 26, 1996

    Joan M. Williams, being duly sworn, deposes and says that he/she resides at 42 Newmarket Street, Wellesely, Norfolk County, Massachusetts, and is the Executor of the Estate of Steven J. Williams, deceased, who died on the 25th day of June, 1996, that at the time of his/her death the domicile of said decedent was at 42 Newmarket Street, Wellesely, Norfolk County, Commonwealth of Massachusetts; that said decedent resided at such address for thirty three (33) years, commencing in 1963; that said decedent last voted in the year 1995, at Norfolk County, Commonwealth of Massachusetts; that the decedent's most recent federal income tax return showed his/her legal residence as 42 Newmarket Street, Wellesely, Massachusetts; that within three years prior to the decedent's death he/she was not a resident of another State; that the securities presented herewith, belonging to the decedent were physically located in the Commonwealth of Massachusetts, on the date of the decedent's death; that all debts and taxes and claims against the decedent's estate have been paid or are being provided for; that this affidavit is made for the purpose of securing the transfer of property owned by the decedent at the time of his death to a person legally entitled thereto under the laws of the decedent's domicile.

Joan M. Williams

Joan M. Williams, Executor

    Then personally appeared the above named Joan M. Williams and acknowledged the foregoing as her free and voluntary act.

John Galt

Notary Public
my commission expires: 9/5/99

July 26, 1996

State Bank
P.O. Box
Boston, MA 02106

Re: Estate of Steven J. Williams
    Account 005969-0000

Dear Sir/Madam:

Please be advised that Steven J. Williams passed away on June 25, 1996 (death certificate enclosed). As Executor/Administrator of this Estate, I am in need of the balance of this account as of the date of death.

Please send this information directly to me:

Joan M. Williams 42 Newmarket Street, Wellesely, MA 02181 (617)555-1234

Additionally, please arrange to have this account closed and a check made payable
to:

Estate of Steven J. Williams, Joan M. Williams, Executor/Administrator

Please forward this check directly me at the address noted above.

Very truly yours,

Joan M. Williams
Executor/Administrator
JOAN M. WILLIAMS

Enclosure

July 26, 1996

Major Mutual Funds
P.O. Box
Boston, MA 02106

attn: Legal Processing Department

Re: Estate of Steven J. Williams
      Account 00223320000

Dear Sir/Madam:

Please be advised that Steven J. Williams passed away on June 25, 1996 and we are presently in the process of collecting all assets owned by Steven J. Williams. I would appreciate your closing the mutual fund account maintained in the decedent's name, and opening a new account in the name of the Estate of Steven J. Williams.

To assist in processing this I am enclosing the following items:

1. Original Death Certificate for Mr. Steven J. Williams;

2. An election notice for federal income tax purposes;

3. Form W-9, Employer Identification Number for the Estate;

4. Certificate of Appointment of Joan M. Williams as ~~Executor~~/Executrix of the estate of Steven J. Williams.

If you have any questions, please contact me.

Very truly yours,

Joan M. Williams
~~Executor~~/Executrix

SIGNATURE GUARANTEED

By: _Albert Albertson_
      (signature)

ALBERT ALBERTSON
      (printed name/title)

Application for Employer Identification Number

Form **SS-4**
(Rev. December 1993)

Department of the Treasury
Internal Revenue Service

(For use by employers, corporations, partnerships, trusts, estates, churches, government agencies, certain individuals, and others. See instructions.)

EIN

OMB No. 1545-0003

Expires 12-31-96

1 Name of applicant (Legal name) (See instructions.) **Estate of Steven J. Williams**	
2 Trade name of business, if different from name in line 1	**3** Executor, trustee, "care of" name **Joan M. Williams, Executor**
4a Mailing address (street address) (room, apt., or suite no.) **42 Newmarket Street,**	**5a** Business address, if different from address in lines 4a and 4b
4b City, state, and ZIP code **Wellesley, MA 02181**	**5b** City, state, and ZIP code
6 County and state where principal business is located **Norfolk County, Ma.**	
7 Name of principal officer, general partner, grantor, owner, or trustor - SSN required (See instructions.) ▶ **Joan M. Williams Exec.**	

8a Type of entity (Check only one box.) (See instructions.)

☐ Sole Proprietor (SSN) _____
☐ REMIC
☐ State/local government
☐ Other nonprofit organization (specify) _____
☐ Other (specify) ▶ _____

☐ Personal service corp.
☐ National guard

☒ Estate (SSN of decedent) **123-45-6789**
☐ Plan administrator-SSN _____
☐ Other corporation (specify) _____
☐ Federal government/military
(enter GEN if applicable) _____

☐ Church or church controlled organization

☐ Trust
☐ Partnership
☐ Farmers' cooperative

8b If a corporation, name the state or foreign country (if applicable) where incorporated ▶   State   Foreign country

9 Reason for applying (Check only one box.)

☐ Started new business (specify) ▶ _____
☐ Hired employees
☐ Created a pension plan (specify type) ▶ _____
☐ Banking purpose (specify) ▶ _____

☐ Changed type of organization (specify) ▶ _____
☐ Purchased going business
☐ Created a trust (specify) ▶ _____
☒ Other (specify) ▶ **Death of S. Williams**

10 Date business started or acquired (Mo., day, year) (See instructions.) **June 25, 1996**

11 Enter closing month of accounting year. (See instructions.) **December 31**

12 First date wages or annuities were paid or will be paid (Mo., day, year). **Note:** If applicant is a withholding agent, enter date income will first be paid to nonresident alien. (Mo., day, year) ▶ **n/a**

13 Enter highest number of employees expected in the next 12 months. **Note:** If the applicant does not expect to have any employees during the period, enter "0." ▶

Nonagricultural	Agricultural	Household
0	0	0

14 Principal activity (See instructions.) ▶ **estate**

15 Is the principal business activity manufacturing?
If "Yes," principal product and raw material used ▶ .... ☐ Yes ☒ No

16 To whom are most of the products or services sold? Please check the appropriate box.
☐ Public (retail) ☐ Other (specify)   ☐ Business (wholesale)   ☒ N/A

17a Has the applicant ever applied for an identification number for this or any other business? .... ☐ Yes ☒ No
Note: If "Yes," please complete lines 17b and 17c.

17b If you checked the "Yes" box in line 17a, give applicant's legal name and trade name, if different than name shown on prior application.
Legal name ▶   Trade name ▶

17c Enter approximate date, city, and state where the application was filed and the previous employer identification number if known.
Approximate date when filed (Mo., day, year)   City and state where filed   Previous EIN

Under penalties of perjury, I declare that I have examined this application, and to the best of my knowledge and belief, it is true, correct, and complete.

Business Telephone number (include area code)

Name and title (Please type or print clearly.) ▶ **Joan M. Williams**

Signature ▶ *Joan M. Williams*   Date ▶ **8/15/96**

Note: Do not write below this line. For official use only.

Please leave blank ▶	Geo.	Ind.	Class	Size	Reason for applying

For Paperwork Reduction Act Notice, see attached instructions.

Form **SS-4** (Rev. 12-93)

H763
4W9012 1.000

Chapter 7
Dealing with Real Estate

General

In Massachusetts real estate owned by the decedent in the person's name alone passes instantly to the heirs or legatees upon death. The executor of the estate has the power to force the sale of the property to pay any necessary expenses or debts, however, this is the only power of the executor. Unless the will of the decedent specifically allows, the legal representative of the estate does not have the power to sell, rent, repair or preserve the property.

Valuation

For purpose of filing the Massachusetts and federal estate tax returns as well as to accurately reflect the value of the real estate on the Inventory, it is often necessary that the real estate owned by the decedent be appraised. There are numerous qualified appraisers who will undertake a physical review of the premises and prepare a report comparing the decedent's property to similar properties sold within the six month period of the death of the decedent. In instances where the real estate is contracted for sale prior to the filing of the estate tax return, then it is common to use the value as negotiated between the willing buyer and the willing seller as the best evidence of fair market value. In such a case it would not be necessary to obtain an appraisal.

Who Owns the Real Estate?

Real estate passes to the inheriting owner, instantly upon the death of the decedent. The legal representative of the estate never obtains true legal title to the property unless the legal representative finds it necessary to sell the real estate to pay necessary debts and expenses of the estate. For this reason, in an estate where there are sufficient assets to satisfy all debts and expenses, the legal representative does not have the authority to rent, mortgage, sell or otherwise deal with the real estate unless a specific directive is provided by the decedent's will. In all other cases the beneficiary of the real estate would be responsible for all maintenance, upkeep and repairs to the property.

Selling the Real Estate

If the decedent's will provides the executor/administrator with the authority to sell or otherwise deal with the decedent's real estate then this "power of sale" will prevent the legal representative from requesting specific legal authority from the probate court. This specific authority is known as a License to Sell Real Estate.

In reviewing a will to determine whether the decedent left the legal representative with a power of sale the following language in some form should appear:

> "I hereby grant to my executor/administrator the power to sell, exchange, lease and to make contracts concerning real property for such considerations and upon such terms as to credit or otherwise as my executor/administrator may determine, and to lease, pledge or mortgage in such manner at such price or on such terms as he/she shall deem advisable, all without the necessity of application to any court, to execute deeds, transfers, leases and other instruments of any kind as well as all other instruments necessary or appropriate in connection with the real estate."

License to Sell Real Estate

In instances where a clear power of sale does not exist in the will, the Massachusetts Conveyancer Title Standards require that the executor/administrator obtain a License to Sell Real Estate from the probate court. There are also instances where the legal representative may elect to obtain a License to Sell Real Estate from the probate court even if a valid power of sale exists in the will. This might be done to ensure that the executor/administrator does not incur any liability or charge that he or she did not obtain the highest price possible for the real estate.

To obtain a License to Sell Real Estate the executor/administrator will file with the probate court a Petition to obtain the license detailing all of the terms and conditions of the negotiated sale of the real estate. Prior to filing the petition, the executor/administrator will have entered into a Purchase and Sale Agreement identifying all terms and conditions of the sale. In all instances when a Petition for a General License to Sell Real Estate is filed it must be filed prior to the expiration of the one year period from the date of the decedent's death. After that time, due to the prevailing rules as to creditors, no further license of the probate court would be required to sell real estate.

If the Petition to Obtain License is accompanied by the written asset of all heirs and interested parties (Devisee and Legatees) then the court upon motion of the executor/administrator should approve the Petition. If the legal representative is unable to obtain all signatures approving of the sale transaction then the probate court would issue a Citation requiring that notice be sent to all people interested in the estate and that the Citation be published in the newspaper.

As with all Citations, once the notice has been provided and the publication has been made the court will wait a stipulated length of time prior to moving forward on the Petition for the License. If no objections are filed, then as a matter of course the court should approve the petition. In cases where an objection is filed by an interested party then the court will hold a hearing to review the merits of the objection.

Estate Tax Issues

Massachusetts Estate Taxes

Massachusetts estate tax law provides that a lien exists on all real estate owned by an individual in Massachusetts at the time of his or her death. This is true of jointly held property as well as property owned individually. Unlike most liens, this lien is not filed in any particular registry of deeds, but rather, it exists as a matter of law. The Massachusetts statute which creates the lien also provides that ten years after the date of death of the decedent the lien is automatically extinguished.

In all cases in which a request is being made of the probate court to issue a License to Sell Real Estate, the probate court requires that evidence be filed indicating that the estate tax lien has been released by the Department of Revenue. The only manner in which the estate tax lien can be released is through the filing of the estate tax return (Form M-706).

There is an expedited system developed by the Department of Revenue to assist in the review of estate tax returns so that lien releases may be issued quickly in cases where real estate is soon to be sold. To do so, requires that the tax return be hand delivered to the Department of Revenue, 215 First Street, Fourth Floor, Cambridge, Massachusetts. There is a daily hearing officer who reviews estate tax returns from 8:45 a.m. to 4:45 p.m. If upon review by the examiner the estate tax return appears accurate as filed then the revenue officer will issue the releases at that time. Two original copies of the releases are provided so that one may be filed with the probate court and one with the registry of deeds.

Federal Estate Taxes

Similar to the Massachusetts system, the federal estate tax system also places a lien on the real estate of a decedent at the time of his or her death. As a practical matter, since the estate of a decedent is not taxable until it reaches a minimum of $600,000.00 and since there is no tax if all assets are passing to a surviving spouse, it is not as often the case that it is necessary to obtain a release of the federal estate tax lien. Massachusetts Conveyancer Standards allow for the use of an Affidavit signed by the executor/administrator of the estate attesting to the fact that there are no federal estate taxes due on the estate.

Purchase and Sale Agreement

As any other person or entity contracting to sell real estate, the estate fiduciary should enter into a signed agreement for purpose of selling the real estate. The Purchase and Sale Agreement should identify the executor/administrator in his or her capacity as the estate fiduciary as follows:

"Joan M. Williams, Executrix of the Estate of Steven J. Williams, and not individually"

If the sale is taking place under a License to Sell Real Estate as issued by the court then information relative to the license should be included in the Purchase and Sale Agreement as follows: "Pursuant to a License to Sell Real Estate as issued by Norfolk County Probate Court, Docket No. P_____".

AFFIDAVIT REGARDING FEDERAL ESTATE TAXES

I, <u>Joan M. Williams</u>, of <u>Wellesley, Norfolk County</u>, Massachusetts, Executor/ Administrator of the Estate of <u>Steven J. Williams</u> who died on <u>June 25</u>, 199<u>6</u> a resident of <u>Wellesley, Norfolk</u> County, Massachusetts (the "Decedent"), do under oath depose and say that the Decedent's gross estate as defined in IRC Section 2031 is less than $ 600,000 and accordingly no federal estate taxes are due and no federal estate tax return will be filed for this estate.

Signed under the pains and penalties of perjury this <u>26th</u> day of <u>July</u>, 199<u>6</u>

Joan M. Williams

Joan M. Williams

COMMONWEALTH OF MASSACHUSETTS

<u>Middlesex</u>, ss. <u>July 26</u>, 199<u>6</u>

Then personally appeared the above-named <u>Joan M. Williams</u> and made oath that the foregoing statement is true and acknowledged the foregoing to be her free act and deed, before me,

_____
Notary Public
My commission expires:

Petition for License to Sell Real Estate

Purpose: This form is used to petition the Court for authority to sell real estate of the decedent.

1) Insert the county in which the decedent was domiciled at time of death.

2) Insert the county in which the decedent was domiciled at time of death.

3) Name of Executor.

4) Name of decedent.

5) Insert the county in which the decedent was domiciled at time of death.

6) Date of appointment as Executor.

7) Insert legal description of property.

8) Insert sale price.

9) The petitioner/executor needs to sign the Petition.

10) All interested parties should sign the Petition to facilitate filing.

Form 17

Commonwealth of Massachusetts
The Trial Court
Probate and Family Court Department

(1) Norfolk _____ Division   Docket No. _____

SALE OF REAL ESTATE

TO THE HONORABLE JUSTICES OF THE PROBATE AND FAMILY COURT IN AND FOR THE COUNTY OF
(2) Norfolk _____ :

RESPECTFULLY represents Joan M. Williams (3)
~~administratrix~~ ~~administrator~~ — executrix — of the will — of Steven J. Williams (4)
(late) of Wellesley
in the County of Norfolk _____, deceased, — ~~testate~~ — ~~intestate~~ —
that ~~he/she/they~~ gave bond for the faithful performance of ~~his/her/their~~ duties on October 1, 1996 (6);
19___; that said deceased was at the time of his/her decease the owner of certain real estate situated in
Wellesley _____, in the County of Norfolk
bounded and described as follows:
(7) Lot 70 of Sidra Gardens Section I
as recorded in plat book 25, page 83 of the public records of
Norfolk County, Massachusetts
_____
_____
the same being — ~~all~~ — part — of the real estate of said deceased.

That it is for the advantage of all parties interested that the same be sold; that an advantageous offer for the purchase of said real estate has been made to the petitioner in the sum of Two Hundred
Thousand (8) dollars.
I — ~~We~~ - certify that the estate of said deceased — does — ~~does not~~ - exceed $1000 in value.

WHEREFORE your petitioner(s) pray(s) that ~~he/she/they~~ may be authorized to sell said real estate of
said deceased — at private sale in accordance with said offer or for a larger sum — ~~at public auction upon~~
~~the following terms:~~

and that he/she/they may become the purchaser(s) of said real estate.

(9) _Joan M. Williams_
Joan M. Williams

Date _____

Date _____

The undersigned, being all persons interested, hereby assent to the foregoing petition.

(10) _James T. Williams_   _Mary K. Williams_
James T. Williams   Mary K. Williams

_____

J-P 76 (8/92)

Commonwealth of Massachusetts
The Trial Court
Probate and Family Court Department

Norfolk Division _____   Docket No. _____

I, ~~We~~, Joan M. Williams ~~administr~~ ~~xxxxxxxxxxxx estate~~ — execut rix of the will — of Steven J. Williams late of Wellesley in the County of Norfolk, deceased — ~~testate~~ — ~~intestate~~ —, the petitioner(s) named in a petition dated October 1, 1996, and on file in said County, praying for authority to sell certain real estate belonging to the estate of said deceased and therein described, do hereby certify under the penalties of perjury that the names of all persons known to — me — ~~us~~ as having or claiming any interest in said real estate derived from any deed or conveyance or mortgage by, through or under any of the — heirs — devisees of said deceased are as follows:

NAME	RESIDENCE	TITLE

Moreover, the petitioner(s) certifies ___ that the Department of Public Welfare is an interested party in this matter due to:

☐ the filing of a written claim against the estate pursuant to M.G.L. ch. 118E, §16A.

☐ the filing of a Notice of Claim pursuant to M.G.L. ch. 197, §9(a).

and request(s) that notice of this petition be sent to the **Department of Public Welfare, P.O. Box 86, Essex Station, Boston, Massachusetts 02112.**

Date October 1, 1996 _____   *Joan M. Williams*
Administrat _____ — Execut rix

Commonwealth of Massachusetts
The Trial Court
Probate and Family Court Department

_____ Division   Docket No. _____

At a Probate and Family Court held at _____, in and for said County of _____ on the _____ day of _____ in the year of our Lord one thousand nine hundred and _____.

On the petition of _____ administrat _____ of the estate — execut _____ of the will — of _____ late of _____ in said County, deceased, — testate — intestate — praying for authority to sell certain real estate of said deceased described in said petition — at private sale, — at public auction, if he/she/they shall think best so to do; all persons interested petition or for a larger sum, or at public auction, if he/she/they shall think best so to do; all persons interested having — assented — been duly notified — and no person objecting thereto, it appearing that said offer is an advantageous one and that the interest of all parties concerned will be best promoted by an acceptance of said offer.

It is expedient to sell real estate of said deceased.

IT IS DECREED that the petitioner(s) be authorized to sell and convey — at public auction — at private sale, upon the following terms:

for the sum of _____ in accordance with said offer or for a larger sum, or at public auction — if he/she/they shall think best so to do, the real estate of said deceased described as follows:

The Commissioner of Corporations and Taxation has released — discharged — the lien on said real estate — and it is further decreed that said petitioner(s) may become the purchaser(s) of said real estate.

_____
Justice of the Probate and Family Court

> *Note: Leave Blank. The Court will fill in this page.*

Chapter 8
Debts and Expenses/Claims of Creditors

General

Once the estate fiduciary has collected all debts and expenses of the decedent and of the estate the executor/administrator needs to determine which of these expenses and claims should be paid. Massachusetts law provides a priority for the payment of expenses and claims as follows:

1. Administrative expenses including court fees, attorneys fees, publication fees, etc.
2. Funeral bills and expenses of decedent's last illness.
3. Federal and State estate taxes.
4. Claims by any municipality or state agency having provided support or care for the decedent.

The duty of the executor/administrator is to review all claims for payment and determine whether they are valid.

Enforcement of Claims Against the Estate

Massachusetts law provides for a one year statute of limitations during which all creditors seeking payment from the estate must assert their rights. In most cases this will mean that a creditor will send notice to the executor/administrator demanding payment of his or her bill or invoice. If the executor/administrator refuses to pay the invoice, then the creditor is confronted with the necessity of needing to file suit to protect themselves from the one year statute of limitations. There is no other formal or informal method for seeking payment from an executor/administrator who refuses to pay a debt. In such case the suit demanding payment must be filed in the district or superior courts and cannot be filed in the probate court.

Chapter 9
Estate Taxes

In General

Estate taxes are taxes levied by the Commonwealth of Massachusetts and the Internal Revenue Service. The estate tax is a transfer type tax on assets transferred by a decedent at the time of death. Since this is a transfer tax, all assets, regardless of the form of ownership (whether joint ownership or owned individually by the decedent) are included in the assets to be taxed. For this reason non-probate assets are often the largest assets being subjected to tax as the non-probate assets of life insurance and retirement plans are included in the estate tax calculations.

While all assets of a decedent are included in the taxable estate, all expenses and debts owed by the decedent are also included. For this reason it is important to track all expenses of the estate to be certain that they are reflected on the estate tax return.

The estate tax return is due to be filed with the IRS and/or the Commonwealth of Massachusetts on the date occurring nine months after the decedent's date of death. It is possible to obtain for cause, extensions on the filing of these returns for up to six months.

Federal Estate Tax

The federal estate tax return is filed in estates where the gross estate exceeds $600,000.00. Since all assets owned by the decedent in whole or in part are included in this calculation, you must be careful to review all non-probate assets to be certain that accurate valuations have been obtained. If the gross estate exceeds $600,000.00 the estate tax return must be filed even though no estate tax is due or payable.

Massachusetts Estate Tax

The Massachusetts estate tax return must be filed in all cases where real estate is a component of the assets being included in the gross estate and in cases where the gross estate exceeds $600,000.00. As of January 1, 1997, the complete phase-out of the Massachusetts estate tax return will have been completed. At that time Massachusetts will become a "sponge tax" state and will receive the estate tax death credit from the Internal Revenue Service for Massachusetts decedents who have filed and paid a federal estate tax.

Chapter 10
Non Resident Decedents/Ancillary Administration

Ancillary Administration refers to the probate court process in Massachusetts for decedents who die domiciled in another state owning real estate and/or tangible personal property in Massachusetts. Under general concepts of probate law, the jurisdiction controlling the probate process and the allowance of a will, is controlled by the state in which the decedent was domiciled at the time of his or her death. Domicile is the decedent's primary and permanent residence.

Generally speaking, the administration of a decedent's intangible personal property is governed by the law of the state in which the decedent was domiciled. Such items as the patent rights, copyrights, royalty rights, etc. are governed by the law of the decedent's domicile. Real estate and tangible personal property owned by a decedent is administered under the law of the state in which the real estate and/or tangible personal property is located.

In circumstances where a decedent died in a jurisdiction other than Massachusetts (i.e., a foreign jurisdiction), leaving real estate and/or tangible personal property in Massachusetts, it will be necessary to perform an ancillary administration in the Commonwealth of Massachusetts. If the foreign executor or administrator does not reside in Massachusetts, then an agent in Massachusetts must be appointed.

To do so will require the use of court documents and papers relating to the probate administration in the state other than Massachusetts. Where a decedent has died testate (with a will) the proper petition is the "Allowance of Foreign Will" Petition. This petition is filed with authenticated or certified copies of the foreign court proceedings. Such items as the petition, bond, will and other probate documents field in the foreign jurisdiction, must be presented to the Massachusetts court. Upon receipt of all necessary documents, the Court will issue a citation to be published in a newspaper in the Commonwealth of Massachusetts. After property compliance with the Order of Notice and the Citation, the Massachusetts court should authorize the named executor to act in Massachusetts for purposes of administering the Massachusetts property.

In a circumstance where a non-Massachusetts domiciliary dies intestate (without a will) once a Petition for Administration in the foreign jurisdiction has been allowed, the foreign administrator will petition the Massachusetts court to administer the decedent's property found in Massachusetts. As in the case of the allowance of a foreign will, the formalities of a bond, military affidavit, and compliance with the requirements of the citation must be adhered to in order to appoint the foreign administrator in the Commonwealth of Massachusetts.

To finalize the ancillary administration of an estate, the foreign fiduciary must close the administration with the filing of an Account covering all actions taken with respect to the Massachusetts property subject to the probate process.

Chapter 11
Closing the Probate Docket

Requirements

Massachusetts Law provides that all estate fiduciaries must account to the Probate Court showing all assets received, funds expended, and any remaining balance of assets left on hand at the time of accounting. Since the fiduciary reports to the court on the Inventory all assets coming into the fiduciary's hands as of a decedent's date of death, the practical purpose of the Account is to track income and expenses from the Inventory, or in the alternative, from the time of the most recent Account. The goal is to provide the interested parties (heirs, legatees, devisees, creditors, etc.) with the information necessary to determine whether the fiduciary's actions as they relate to the estate have been proper.

Massachusetts law does not provide a time frame within which an account must be filed. For this reason, it is not uncommon to have accounts filed for lengthy periods of time covering one, two or more years. As will be discussed later, it is often preferable to account more frequently so that issues relating to the account period can be challenged or assented to, thereby closing those issues.

Content and Format of Accounts

In essence, the basic requirement is that each account of an estate fiduciary contain three schedules. Schedule A will contain all receipts received by the fiduciary. Schedule B will contain all expenditures made by the fiduciary. Schedule C will contain the balance on hand in the estate, if any, at the end of the period of the account. When a Final Account is prepared, Schedule C will always have a zero balance as no assets will be remaining on hand.

In preparing an account, while not a statutory requirement, it is suggested that the account be structured to provide for easy review by those to whom it will be presented. For this reason, grouping transactions by common elements, common dates, or numbering transactions will serve to make the account easier to review. With the use of word processing software, the stylistic preparation of an account has become much easier.

The preparation of the account must be viewed from the point of view of a lay person who will either assent or contest the account. This review of the account may be the first and only time an interested person has any information regarding the estate's assets. For this reason, every number and item listed on an account must be clearly stated, with a minimum of abbreviations, be accurate, defensible and documented so that upon questions or challenge, the accountant (the estate fiduciary) may properly explain and defend the items listed. It is not uncommon for an account to be challenged, not because of the content of the account, but rather, because of confusing presentation or mislabeling of dates. Substantial litigation and delay can be avoided by accurately detailing dates of transactions and isolating key elements to a large transaction.

Schedule A — Receipts

The purpose of Schedule A is to detail all items coming into the hands of the fiduciary since the date of the Inventory or the date of the most recent account. The items typically included on Schedule A are items in the nature of "income" earned by the estate. Items such as interest, dividends, refunds of various assets owned by the decedent, income due the decedent at the date of death but not paid until some later point in time, gains on sales of estate assets, etc. Additionally, items that have come into the hands of the fiduciary since the date of the prior account or the date of the Inventory should also be listed. This can very typically be estate assets which have been uncovered and discovered since the filing of the Inventory.

Schedule B — Expenditures

Schedule B of the account is designed to account for all expenditures made by the fiduciary during the period of administration. Additionally, losses on estate asset transactions, as well as refunds paid and the return of assets which are not properly attributable to the estate (i.e., refund of social security checks and disability income checks) would be reflected on Schedule B if included on the Inventory. Items such as funeral bills, debts and expenses of the decedent, any expenses of administration (i.e., attorney's fees, accounting fees, probate court fees, publication fees, etc.), all legacies and final distribution of estate assets to the heirs or legatees must be reflected on Schedule B.

Schedule C — Remaining Balance

Schedule C of the account will reflect either the balance remaining on hand which is subject to continuing administration, or a zero balance in the event it is a "Final" account. For estates which will take several years to administer, it is common for a fiduciary to prepare and file an account for a convenient period of time (i.e., twelve months, or a calendar year). In such instances, the value of assets on Schedule A less the expenditures on Schedule B will total the remaining assets on hand in Schedule C. In preparing the next account, the accountant (estate fiduciary) will begin the account with the balance remaining in Schedule C from the prior account.

As a practical matter, the estate fiduciary can often be caught in a bind between the probate court and the persons inheriting the estate assets. In preparing an account, it is necessary that the fiduciary obtain approval from all interested parties and heirs at law indicating that the administration of the estate has been properly undertaken. To do so will require that the fiduciary distribute all assets remaining to the appropriate heirs or legatees. A problem can arise when the fiduciary distributes assets to a purported heir only to learn that he may have incorrectly paid estate assets to the wrong person or that a challenge is made to the account.

Alternatively, heirs and legatees may not be willing to sign an account until they have been paid the amounts that are due them. For this reason, shortly before finalizing the estate, estate fiduciaries may sometime prepare an account reflecting all estate transactions, including a partial distribution to the estate legatees and heirs at law. This account would be presented for approval by all interest persons and filed for allowance by the probate court. Once approved, all transactions in the account would be final. This will allow the fiduciary to prepare a Final Account running from the date of the earlier account to final distribution of the estate. This Final Account will contain few, if any, transactions other than reflecting the final distribution of assets to the heirs. This may assist the fiduciary in dealing with this "catch-22" of estate heirs requesting their assets prior to assenting to any fiduciary account.

Filing and Allowance of Accounts

Fees

Under Massachusetts General Laws a fiduciary appointed by the Probate and Family Court Department must, as a condition of his or her probate bond, file an account annually. Similar to other time requirements, there is no penalty for failure to meet this time constraint. This being the case, accounts often cover more than one year of time, especially in small estates which are fully administered in a period of time less than two years. In such a case, the fiduciary may choose to prepare a "First and Final Account" to cover the entire period of estate administration. For this reason the court fees for filing of an account reflect a fee per each year or major fraction thereof. The present filing fees are as follows:

Gross Value of Schedule A	Filing Fee per year or major fraction of a year
$ 1,000.00 - or less	No Fee
$ 1,001.00 - $ 9,999.00	$ 30.00 per year
$ 10,000.00 - $ 100,000.00	$ 50.00 per year
$ 100,000.00 - $ 500,000.00	$ 70.00 per year
$ 500,000.00 - $1,000,000.00	$ 100.00 per year
$ 1,000,000.00 - or more	$ 200.00 per year

It is suggested that the paralegal contact the court or review the schedule in Massachusetts Lawyer's Diary or similar volume to obtain the most recent schedule of fees.

Filing Requirements

While Massachusetts law requires that an account be filed annually, there is no requirement that an account be presented for allowance. The phrase "presented for allowance" refers to the process of having the account reviewed by the court and adhering to all of the procedures necessary in having all appropriate parties notified of the account, review and if appropriate, approve of the account. A fiduciary will not be released from his or her court bond until such time as a Final Account has been allowed by the court. Because the presentation of an account for allowance and the allowance itself will serve to cut off rights of those who object to the account, a process and set of procedures have been established to insure that all interested persons have an opportunity to review and if necessary object to the account.

Steps for Allowance

Massachusetts Laws detail those persons to whom specific notice of the account must be rendered. If those persons or entities review the account and execute a written assent to the account, then the court may allow the account without any further requirement of notice or publication. In the event the accountant cannot secure the written assent of all interested persons and heirs as requirement under the statutes, then the court will issue a citation.

As with all citations issued by the court, the citation will provide a summary of the matter at hand and an order requirement notification via publication and mailing to certain persons. The citation will also contain a return date at which time any person objecting to the account must have filed a written objection. Absent any written objections and an adherence to the requirements of the citation, after the return date has passed the court should allow the account.

Mailing

The citation will direct that a copy of the citation be delivered or mailed at least fourteen days prior to the return date. It is often best to send these notices certified mail/return receipt requested to insure that you can establish having properly complied with the notice requirement. It is imperative that the fourteen day period be adhered to strictly. The court will typically provide a four to five week time frame between the issuance of the citation and the return date and accordingly there should be sufficient time to forward this notice to the relevant parties.

Publication

In addition to the mailing requirement discussed above, the law requires that the citation be published "unless all persons interested receive actual notice". For this reason in instances where all interested persons and heirs at law assent to the account, it will not be necessary to publish the citation.

It is imperative that the notice be published in the newspaper chosen by the court in the citation. This will be found in the lower portion of the citation detailing the time frame within which the publication must be made. It is suggested that the newspaper be requested to forward a proof of the publication prior to printing so that any typographical errors made be uncovered.

Once published, a tear sheet (an actual page from the newspaper containing the notice) should be obtained from the newspaper for purposes of final review of the content of the notice and to be retained in the file to establish that proper publication was undertaken.

The Return

Once notice has been properly mailed to the necessary parties and been published in the appropriate newspaper, the fiduciary, or the attorney on the fiduciary's behalf, may complete the citation. To do so, the phrase "publishing and mailing as directed" should be inserted in the lower portion of the citation. This should be signed by the fiduciary or the attorney and returned to the court prior to or on the return date.

Charities

In cases where a charity is involved in the administration of an estate, it is necessary that notice of the account be filed with the Attorney General's office of the Commonwealth of Massachusetts. It is common to include in the notification package to the Attorney General's office a copy of the entire account.

Guardian Ad Litem

If there are beneficiaries of the estate who are unborn, unascertained, or legally incompetent to act on their own behalf (including minors), the court shall appoint a Guardian Ad Litem to represent such interest. It is imperative that the estate fiduciary determine whether a Guardian Ad Litem is necessary or the account and its allowance will not be binding on those who were not properly notified.

Typically a Guardian Ad Litem is appointed when a minor has interests in the estate and has no other legally appointed guardian protecting their interests.

A review of the decedent's will should be undertaken to determine whether the decedent specifically requested that a Guardian Ad Litem be dispensed with as it relates to unborn or unascertained persons. Absent a compelling reason, the court will typically dispense with any such Guardian Ad Litem appointment for unascertained or unborn persons. It is not however possible to waive the requirement of a Guardian Ad Litem where minors or other incompetents are not properly represented by others other than the accountant.

Documents Necessary to Present an Account for Allowance

In addition to the filing of an original account signed by the estate fiduciary, the following items must be filed with the account for the court to have the account presented for allowance:

Military Affidavit

The Military Affidavit detailing any persons in the military service of the United States or its allies must be prepared and signed by the fiduciary or the fiduciary's attorney prior to the allowance of the account.

Estate Tax Closing Letter

Letter from the Department of Revenue evidencing that payment of all estate taxes due and owing the Commonwealth of Massachusetts must be obtained and filed prior to the allowance of the account.

A Judgement for Use by the Probate Court in Allowing the Account

Due to the restraints on the resources of the probate courts, it is now a requirement that the accountant provide a form judgement prepared for signature by a judge when filing the account. If the account is allowed, the judge will then sign the judgement form provided.

Written Assents

If obtained, all written assents should be filed with the account at the time of presentation for allowance.

Transmittal Letter

In presenting the necessary documents to the court, it is important that the cover letter express the fiduciary's wish that this account be presented for allowance. As indicated, accounts can be filed and not presented for allowance. In such a case the account will be filed in the probate docket and no further action will be taken by the court.

To prevent unnecessary delay in instances where an account should be presented for allowance, it is imperative that the representative request in the letter transmitting the documents that the probate court "present the account for allowance". By doing so the court will, if all assents are attached, present the account for allowance, or if all assents are not attached, issue a citation to the fiduciary. It is not uncommon for accounts to be filed without a directive to be presented for allowance. This will result in no action being taken by the court and thereby causing several months of delay and embarrassment on behalf of the fiduciary.

Contesting an Account

If an account is filed without all necessary parties assenting, the court will issue a citation providing an opportunity for interested persons to review and if necessary object to the account. The mechanics for objecting to an account are governed by Massachusetts Rules of Civil Procedure, Rule 72.

Under Rule 72, any person objecting to an account must file a written appearance with the court before the return date indicating their objection to the account. Any person interested or affected by the account has the right to file any such objection. Within thirty (30) days of the return date, the objecting party must file with the court a written statement of objections to the items on the account to which the person is objecting. If no such written statement is filed, then the estate fiduciary may bring a motion to strike the objection and to have the account allowed.

Rule 72, provides a clear detail items of discover, etc. that are allowed for purposes of the objection to the account. Once an objection has been filed, either party (the objecting party or the fiduciary) may mark the matter for hearing before the court relating to those items objected to in the objection. As in all matters of litigation, only a party with proper standing may file an appearance against an account. For this reason the governing statute addresses the account to only persons "having an interest affected by the account".

Appeal of Allowed Account

Once an account has been allowed, General Law Chapter 206 §24 provides that an account shall not be impeached except for fraud or manifest error. Circumstances in which fraud or manifest error have been found are few and far between. As a practical matter, absent extraordinary circumstances or errors, a properly allowed account will not be re-opened by the court.

Account

Purpose: The Account is a detailed accounting of all financial transactions by an estate fiduciary.

1) County of decedent's domicile at date of death.

2) Insert the appropriate number Account (i.e. First Account, Second Account, or Final Account).

3) Name of estate fiduciary.

4) Type of estate fiduciary.

5) The period of the accounting.

6) Amounts received by the estate fiduciary.

7) Amounts expended by the estate fiduciary.

8) Balance of assets remaining in the fiduciary's hands.

9) Signature line for estate fiduciary.

10) Signatures of all interested parties assenting to the Account.

Form 18

Commonwealth of Massachusetts
The Trial Court
Probate and Family Court Department

Docket No. _____

Account

(1) Norfolk **Division**

(2) First _____ Account of (3) Joan M. Williams
and _____
as (4) Executrix
_____
(Specify type of fiduciary and name of estate)

This account is for the period of (5) July 15, 1996, to July 15, 1997
(date)
inclusive.

Principal amounts received per Schedule A   (6) $ 403,048.25

Principal payments and charges per Schedule B   (7) $ 378,048.25

Principal balance invested per Schedule C   (8) $ 25,000.00
Market value as of July 15, 1997 per Schedule C $ _____
(date)

Income received per Schedule D $ _____

Payments from income per Schedule E $ _____

Income balance per Schedule F $ _____

The United States Veterans' Administration is - is not - a party in interest to this account. The ward is not a patient in a State hospital.

I certify under the penalties of perjury that the within account is just and true.

(9) _Joan M. Williams_
Joan M. Williams

Signature of Fiduciary

Date _____

The undersigned, being all persons _____ interested, having examined the foregoing account, request that the same may be allowed without further notice.

(10) _Joan M. Williams_
Joan M. Williams

Mary K. Williams
Mary K. Williams

James T. Will
James T. Williams

CJ-P 30 (8/88)

ESTATE OF STEVEN J. WILLIAMS

NORFOLK COUNTY PROBATE COURT

DOCKET NUMBER 96P

ACCOUNT

SCHEDULE A

Personal Estate per Inventory $ 292,001.00

A. Bank Interest Income
- 07/30/96 $ 10.13
- 08/31/96 $ 36.44
- 09/30/96 $ 26.77
- 10/29/96 $ 179.14
- 11/30/96 $ 153.33
- 12/31/96 $ 66.87
- 01/31/97 $ 81.51
- 02/28/97 $ 94.06
- 03/31/97 $ 104.14

Total Interest Income $ 752.39

B. Investment Account - Interest Income
- 11/19/96 $ 37.83
- 12/31/96 $ 27.28
- 01/31/97 $ 695.42
- 02/28/97 $ 754.08
- 03/31/97 $ 328.99

Total Interest Income $ 1,843.60

C. 02/22/96 - National Life Assurance $ 65.00

D. 02/25/96 - National Assocation of City Employees $ 2,250.00

E. 05/01/96 - Social Security $ 939.00

F. 05/05/96 - Time, Inc. Magazine Refund $ 6.23

G. 05/20/96 - Household Credit Services Refund $ 25.00

H. 10/30/96 - Bank Interest $ 100.00

I. 11/18/96 Sale proceeds, 14 Jones Street Norfolk, Ma. $ 96,360.79

J. 09/09/96 Equitable Life Assurance Company Interest Income $ 4,297.68

K. 10/6/96 Fleet Bank Account Interest Income $ 461.00

L. 01/18/97 Fidelity IRA - Increase in Value over Inventory Value $ 3,196.56

M. 03/15/97 Final disability insurance payment $ 750.00

TOTAL SCHEDULE A $ 403,048.25

ESTATE OF STEVEN J. WILLIAMS

NORFOLK COUNTY PROBATE COURT

DOCKET NUMBER 96P

ACCOUNT - Schedule B

Charges to Principal

1.	Accounting Expenses 8/6/97	$ 54.58
2.	Legal Expenses	
	8/6/96	$ 1,941.80
	11/11/96	$ 2,556.40
	1/30/97	$ 1,442.00
	3/31/97	$ 2,675.00
3.	Funeral Expense 8/6/96	$ 8,186.60
4.	Flowers 3/23/96	$ 1,159.00
5.	Kaminsky Appraisal Services - 8/6/96	$ 325.00
6.	Norfolk County Probate Court	
	- 7/9/96 - Filing Fees	$ 90.00
	- 7/9/96 - Certificates of Appointment	$ 50.00
	- 8/9/96 - Courier Fees	$ 15.00
	- 3/31/97- Account Fee	$ 70.00
7.	Executrix Fee 3/31/97	$ 6,000.00
8.	Massachusetts Department of Revenue Estate Tax - Allocable Portion to Residuary Estate	$ 16,234.02
9.	Bank Service Charges	$ 91.35
10	Citibank Visa	$ 980.00
11.	Medical Group, Inc. - 3/31/97	$ 110.00

12.	Reduction in value of Tangible Personal Property. Proceeds of sale - $717.00 Inventory Value $2,440.00	$ 1,723.00
13.	Joan Williams - Distribution of proceeds from sale of real estate	$ 96,360.79
14.	Joan Williams - Distribution pursuant to Article IV of the Last Will and Testament.	$ 142,790.23
15.	James Williams - Distribution pursuant to Article IV of the Last Will and Testament.	$ 23,798.37
16.	John Williams - Distribution pursuant to Article IV of the Last Will and Testament	$ 23,798.37
17.	Steven Carter - Distribution pursuant to Article IV of the Last Will and Testament.	$ 23,798.37
18.	Mary K. Williams - Distribution pursuant to Article IV of the Last Will and Testament.	$ 23,798.37
	Total Schedule B	$ 378,048.25

ESTATE OF STEVEN J. WILLIAMS

NORFOLK PROBATE DOCKET 96P

ACCOUNT - SCHEDULE C

PRINCIPAL BALANCE INVESTED

Bank Checking Account $ 25,000.00

TOTAL SCHEDULE C $ 25,000.00

Judgment

Purpose: The Judgment is the document signed by the Judge of the probate court allowing the Account of the estate fiduciary.

1) County of decedent's death.

2) Name of estate.

3) Town in which the probate court is situated.

4) The type of Account being filed.

5) Name of estate fiduciary.

6) Name of estate.

7) Address of decedent at time of death.

8) Name of estate fiduciary.

Form 19

Commonwealth of Massachusetts
The Trial Court
Probate and Family Court Department

(1) Norfolk Division

Docket No. _____

Judgment

Estate of (2) Steven J. Williams

At the Probate and Family Court held at (3) Dedham

in and for said County, on _____ November _____, 19 96 .

The (4) First and Final account(s) of (5) Joane M. Williams ,

Executrix

of the estate of (6) Steven J. Williams ,

(late) of (7) 42 Newmarket Street, Wellesley Norfolk 02181
(street and no.)   (city or town)   (county)   (zip)

The said account(s) of said, (8) Joan M. Williams, Executor

having been presented for allowance, and certified by the accountant — ~~and~~

~~the guardian ad litem~~ — and all persons interested — having been duly notified — having consented thereto in writing, and no objections being made thereto, and the same having been examined and considered by the Court.

It is ordered and adjudged that said account(s) be allowed.

_____
Date

_____
Justice of the Probate and Family Court

CJ-P 38 (1/89)

72

Chapter 12
Payment of Legacies
Distribution of Intestate Property

In distributing the assets of an estate, the estate fiduciary must use caution to distribute the assets in a timely fashion, giving great thought to the risk inherent in distributing assets too soon. As a general rule, given the current provisions of Massachusetts Law controlling the one year period during which a creditor may assert his or her claim against the estate, an estate fiduciary cannot safely pay out the assets of the estate until the one year creditor claim period has been exhausted. For this reason, it is often common not to distribute estate assets until the one year period from date of death has expired.

Payment of Legacies

In cases where a decedent's will provided for the distribution of tangible personal property to specific persons, the payment of these legacies should be made upon the expiration of the one year creditor claim period. For decedent's dying on or after January 1, 1990, interest on legacies began to run commencing on the one year anniversary of the decedent's date of death. Again for this reason, the legacy should be distributed promptly at the one year period.

Similar to diarying the nine month due date of the estate tax return, it is prudent to diary the one year anniversary for both the extinguishment of creditor claims as well as the distribution of legacies.

Whenever an estate fiduciary distributes legacies, it is imperative that the fiduciary receives a written assent acknowledging the receipt by the legatee of the legacy and the satisfaction of that provision of the will. In the event the estate fiduciary is distributing legacies prior to the expiration of the one year period, some form of an indemnification agreement should be obtained from the person receiving the legacy to insure that the executor is not personally exposed should creditor claims arise after the date of distribution of the legacy.

In distributing the residuary estate, Massachusetts law does not require the payment of the residuary estate within any specific time frame. Rather, the requirement is that the residuary estate be distributed in a reasonable amount of time. It is this distribution of the residuary estate that often leads to unnecessary conflict between the heirs and the estate fiduciary. It is best to inform the persons inheriting the residuary estate that no such distribution will be undertaken within at least the first year after the date of death. This final distribution may take substantially longer depending on the complexity of the estate and issues relating to income and estate tax return filings, creditor claims, etc.

Real Estate

In circumstances where a decedent died intestate, title to the real estate vests in the heirs of the decedent at the date of death. The ownership of the heirs is subject however to the power of an administrator to sell the real estate in order to pay debts and expenses. Since the real estate is instantly vested in the heirs subject to the rights of the administrator to sell the real estate, as a practical matter it is unnecessary for the administrator to transfer the real estate to the heirs. Once the one year creditor period has elapsed, the heirs of the decedent may deal freely with the real estate.

In testate circumstances, title to the real estate vests in the devisee upon the allowance of the will and relates back to the date of death of the decedent.

Payment of Legacies to Minors

If estate assets are to be distributed to a minor, the estate fiduciary must pay the inheritance to either the properly appointed guardian of the minor; deposit the assets with the Probate and Family Court Department; or in circumstances where the bequest is less than $10,000.00 the amount may be distributed under the Uniform Transfers to Minors Act through the use of a custodian.

RECEIPT FOR DISTRIBUTION

I, _____Andy Williams_____, of _____Newton_____ Massachusetts hereby acknowledge receipt of $_____5,000_____ from the Estate of _____Steven J. Williams_____,
_____Joan M. Williams_____, Administrator, as a partial distribution from the Estate. In
consideration of said distribution the undersigned hereby agrees as follows:

1. That this distribution is made upon the condition that the assets of the estate of
    _____Steven J. Williams_____ remaining in the hands of the Administrator after this
    distribution, shall be sufficient to pay all of the debts and claims properly payable by the
    Administrator, to reimburse him for his expenses and to pay any federal, state or local
    tax payable by the executor, and

2. That I will indemnify the Administrator and hold him harmless from any debts, claims,
    expenses or taxes properly payable by him to the extent, if any, that the assets remaining
    in the said estate after this distribution shall be insufficient therefore, but not in excess
    of the amount of said distribution, and

3. That I, without further notice, hereby assent to any and all accounts of
    said_____Joan M. Williams_____ as Administrator of the Estate of
    _____Steven J. Williams_____ that reflects said distribution to me.

Dated this _1st_ day of _____August_____, 199_6_

Andy Williams

Social Security No. _____039-99-9999_____

Glossary

Beneficiary(ies)

A person or persons named in a will, or benefiting from an estate where there is no will, who inherits assets of the decedent.

Bond

A written promise/guarantee to the probate court that the individual requesting to be named as the fiduciary will faithfully undertake the duties in accordance with Massachusetts law.

Certificate of Appointment

A certificate prepared by the Probate Court attesting to the fact that the executor or administrator has been appointed and is presently authorized to undertake actions on behalf of the estate.

Creditor

An individual or entity to whom money may be owed by either the decedent or the estate.

Decedent

The person who has passed away.

Devisee

A person who inherits real estate from a decedent who specifically listed the gift in his will.

Heir

A person who by law is entitled to inherit the assets of another person.

Intestate

Passing away without a will.

Inventory

A list of all assets that a decedent owned at the time of death, in the person's name alone.

Legatee

A person who inherits personal property through a decedent's will.

Letters of Administration

This document, in Massachusetts, is the same document as the Certificate of Appointment wherein the court indicates that the individual is authorized to undertake actions on behalf of the estate.

Petition

A Petition is a formal request in writing of the probate court to undertake a particular action, most typically to begin the probate process.

Petitioner

The person who files the Petition with the court requesting that they be appointed as the estate fiduciary.

Probate

The court process to settle an individual's estate and distribute the assets owned by an individual in their name alone.

Resident Agent

In instances where the executor does not reside in the Commonwealth of Massachusetts, the resident agent is an individual within the Commonwealth of Massachusetts who is designated as the person to be responsible to receive any notice or service of summons in the estate.

Testate

Passing away with a will.

Testator/Testatrix

Male or Female who created the last will and testament.

Appendix A
Probate Checklist

WHEN: IMMEDIATELY AFTER DEATH

1.   Locate any last will and testament of the decedent. If a will can't be found, be certain all locations have been reviewed to eliminate the possibility of the will appearing after filing an administration.

2.   Obtain several certified copies of the death certificate.

3.   (a)   If there is a will then file with probate court the following:

   1.   Original Last Will and Testament
   2.   Petition for Probate
   3.   Certified copy of death certificate
   4.   Bond
   5.   Military Affidavit (if all heirs have not assented)
   6.   Appointment of Agent (for appointment of non-Massachusetts executor)

   (b)   If there is no will then to commence the administration the following should be filed with the appropriate probate court:

   1.   Petition for Probate
   2.   Certified copy of death certificate
   3.   Bond
   4.   Military Affidavit (if all heirs have not assented)
   5.   Appointment of Agent (for appointment of non-Massachusetts executor)

4.   Send a copy of the Death Certificate and the Petition to Probate to the Department of Public Welfare.

5.   If the decedent was receiving Social Security, contact the Social Security Administration to notify them of the decedent's death so that any future payments will cease.

6.   Begin collecting all information about assets and liabilities and organize them into separate folders.

7.   Review any homeowner's insurance involved to be sure the property is insured in the event it is now unoccupied.

WHEN: **UPON RECEIPT OF CITATION FROM PROBATE COURT**

1. Review citation to determine who receives notice and what newspaper notice must be published in.

2. Contact the newspaper to obtain information about scheduling the publication of the legal notice.

3. Mail a copy of the citation to all interested parties (legatees, devisees and heirs who have not assented to the Petition) as directed in the Citation.

4. Upon receipt of the tear sheet from the newspaper, proof the printed legal notice to be certain that it has been printed verbatim.

5. Prior to or on the return date as specified in the citation, make return to the probate court as required in the citation.

6. If no objection has been filed, then the clerk should be able to provide you information as to how long before the court will approve the petition and name the executor/administrator.

WHEN: **IMMEDIATELY AFTER APPOINTMENT**

1. Obtain a federal tax identification number (Form SS-4).

2. Open an estate checking account.

3. Gather all assets and asset records of the estate, such as:

   - bank statements
   - pass books
   - mutual fund and securities statements
   - savings bonds
   - car titles
   - prior year's tax returns, etc.

4. Send letters to all creditors to have them forward all invoices directly to the executor/administrator.

5. File any necessary claims forms to collect the benefits of any life insurance policies payable to the estate.

WHEN: **WITHIN THREE MONTHS OF APPOINTMENT**

1. Begin valuing all assets and estimating the total of expenses.

2. Begin preparation of any necessary estate tax returns.

3. Arrange for professional appraisals of real estate and tangible property if necessary.

4. Determine whether ancillary administration is necessary due to assets owned in another state.

5. Prepare probate Inventory and file with the probate court. There is no filing fee for the filing of the Inventory.

WHEN: **WITHIN FOUR MONTHS AFTER APPOINTMENT**

If the estate is solvent then the administrator/executor may begin paying debts.

1. Pay priority expenses of funeral bill, and other preferred expenses first. If the estate is insolvent the fiduciary should render the estate insolvent.

WHEN: **WITHIN SIX MONTHS AFTER DATE OF DEATH**

1. Re-value all assets of the estate for purpose of determining whether the alternate valuation date of six months after date of death will be used for estate tax purposes.

WHEN: **WITHIN SIX MONTHS AFTER APPOINTMENT**

1. The surviving spouse must determine within six months of the appointment of the executor or administrator whether he or she will be claiming the statutory share.

WHEN: **NINE MONTHS AFTER DEATH**

1. Federal and Massachusetts estate tax returns must be filed.

2. Any disclaimers to be filed with the probate court must be filed on or before nine months from date of death.

WHEN: **ONE YEAR AFTER DATE OF DEATH**

Last day for creditors to file claims against the estate.

WHEN: **WITHIN ONE YEAR AFTER APPOINTMENT**

Any petition of the probate court for License to Sell Real Estate must be filed within one year of the appointment of the executor/administrator.

WHEN: **WITHIN FIFTEEN MONTHS AFTER DATE OF DEATH**

Any necessary fiduciary income tax returns should be filed.

WHEN: **WITHIN THIRTY DAYS OF RECEIPT OF ESTATE TAX CLOSING LETTER**

1.   If a federal closing letter is received than it must be filed with the Massachusetts Estate Tax Bureau.

2.   Pay any additional taxes assessed on the closing letter.

3.   Record any Release of Estate Tax Liens (Form M-792).

4.   File the Massachusetts Estate Tax Closing Letter with the probate court.

5.   File any final fiduciary income tax returns that may be due.

6.   Make final distribution of estate assets to heirs (maintaining a reserve for final expenses).

7.   Prepare and file Final Account with probate court.

8.   Have the Final Account allowed by the probate court.

9.   Notify any corporate surety of the allowance of the probate Account.

Appendix B
Forms

Chapter 1
-   Form 1   Voluntary Executor/Executrix
-   Form 2   Voluntary Administration

Chapter 2
-   Form 3   Probate of Will with/without Sureties
-   Form 4   Declination
-   Form 5   General Assent
-   Form 6   Appointment of Agent
-   Form 7   Military Affidavit

Chapter 3
-   Form 8   Administration with/without Sureties
-   Form 9   Probate of Will-Administration with the will annexed with/without sureties
-   Form 10   Special Administration

Chapter 4
-   Form 11   Bond

Chapter 6
-   Form 12   Affidavit of Domicile
-   Form 13   Notice to Bank
-   Form 14   Notice to Mutual Funds Co.
-   Form 15   Application for employer I.D. Number

Chapter 7
-   Form 16   Affidavit Regarding Federal Estate Taxes
-   Form 17   Sale of Real Estate

Chapter 11
-   Form 18   Account
-   Form 19   Judgment

Chapter 12
-   Form 20   Receipt for Distribution

Commonwealth of Massachusetts
The Trial Court
Probate and Family Court Department

_____ **Division**

Docket No. _____

Voluntary Executor/Executrix

Name of Decedent _____

Domicile at Death _____

(Street and No.)   (City or Town)   (County)   (Zip)

Date of Death _____

Will and Death Certificate shall be filed with application.

Name and address of Applicant(s) _____

_____ Status _____

Your Applicant(s) respectfully state(s) that said estate consisting entirely of personal property the total value of which does not exceed fifteen thousand dollars ($15,000) exclusive of the decedent's automobile as shown by the following schedule of all the assets of said deceased known to the applicant(s):

Name of Property	Estimated Value
_____	$ _____
_____	$ _____
_____	$ _____
_____	$ _____
_____	$ _____
_____ **Total**	$ _____

That thirty days have expired since the date of death of said deceased and no petition for probate of will or appointment of administration/administratrix has been filed in said Court.

That your applicant(s) ha ___ undertaken to act as voluntary executor/executrix of the estate of said deceased and will administer the same according to law and apply the proceeds thereof in conformity with Section 16A of Chapter 195 of the General Laws.

That to the knowledge of the applicant(s) the following are the names and addresses of all persons surviving who, with the deceased, were joint owners of property; also listed are the names and addresses of those who would take under the provisions of Section 3 of Chapter 190 in the case of intestacy, and the names and addresses of those who would take under the provisions of the will.

_____

_____

_____

_____

_____

☐ The applicant(s) hereby certif _____ that a copy of this document, along with a copy of the decedent's death certificate has been sent by <u>certified mail</u> to the **Department of Public Welfare, P.O. Box 86, Essex Station, Boston, Massachusetts 02112.**

Date _____   Signature _____

NOTARIZATION

_____ ss   Date _____

Then personally appeared _____
to me known and made oath that the information contained in the foregoing statement is true to the best of his/her/their knowledge and belief.

Before me, _____

NOTARY PUBLIC/JUSTICE OF THE PEACE

My Commission expires _____

CJ-P7A (8/92)

For Petitioner:

_____

_____

Voluntary Executor

Statement

Filed _____ 19 ____

Attested Copy Issued _____ 19 ____

Recorded Vol. _____ Page _____

Instructions

Refer to Massachusetts General Laws Chapter 195, Section 16A, as amended.

Will and Death certificate must be filed with application.

Give motor vehicle identification number.

Status of applicant includes the following:

surviving spouse, child, grandchild, parent, brother, sister, niece, nephew, aunt or uncle if of full age and legal capacity and inhabitant of the Commonwealth of Massachusetts.

Notice Regarding Massachusetts Estate Taxes

You may need to file a Massachusetts Estate Tax Return and a Massachusetts Fiduciary Income Tax Return, especially if the decedent owned an interest in real estate, or if the decedent had more than $100 of income received after the date of death.

You may need to file a Massachusetts Estate Tax Return (Form M-706) in order to obtain a release of lien (Form M-792) on this real estate.

You may need to file a Massachusetts Fiduciary Income Tax Return (Form 2) to report income of more than $100 received after the date of death.

You should contact the Massachusetts Estate Tax Bureau for information and assistance regarding the estate tax law (617-727-4448) or the fiduciary income tax law (617-727-4305).

Commonwealth of Massachusetts
The Trial Court
Probate and Family Court Department

_____ Division   **Docket No.** _____

Voluntary Administration

Name of Decedent _____

Domicile at Death _____
　　　　　　　　　　　(Street and No.)　　　　　　　　　(City or Town)　　　(County)　　(Zip)

Date of Death_____

Death Certificate shall be filed with application.

Name and address of Applicant(s) _____

_____ Status _____

Your applicant(s) respectfully state(s) that said estate consisting entirely of personal property the total value of which does not exceed fifteen thousand dollars ($15,000) exclusive of the decedent's automobile as shown by the following schedule of all the assets of said deceased known to the applicant(s):

Name of Property	**Estimated Value**
_____	$_____
_____	$_____
_____	$_____
_____	$_____
_____	$_____
_____ **Total**	$_____

That thirty days have expired since the date of death of said deceased and no petition for probate of will or appointment of administration/administratrix has been filed in said Court.

That your applicant(s) ha____undertaken to act as voluntary administrator/administratrix of the estate of said deceased and will administer the same according to law and apply the proceeds thereof in conformity with Section 16 of Chapter 195 of the General Laws.

That to the knowledge of the applicant(s) the following are the names and addresses of all persons surviving who, with the deceased, were joint owners of property: also listed are the names and addresses of those who would take under the provisions of Section 3 of Chapter 190 in the case of intestacy.

_____

_____

_____

☐ The applicant(s) hereby certif _____that a copy of this document, along with a copy of the decedent's death certificate has been sent by <u>certified mail</u> to the **Department of Public Welfare, P.O. Box 86, Essex Station, Boston, Massachusetts 02112.**

Date _____   Signature _____

NOTARIZATION

_____ , ss.   Date _____ , 19____

Then personally appeared_____
to me known and made oath that the information contained in the foregoing statement is true to the best of his/her/their knowledge and belief.

Before me,_____
　　　　　　　NOTARY PUBLIC/JUSTICE OF THE PEACE

My Commission expires_____

CJ-P7 (8/92)

For Petitioner:

_____

_____

Docket No. _____

Voluntary Administration
Statement

Filed _____ 19____

Attested Copy Issued _____ 19____

Recorded Vol. _____ Page _____

Instructions

Refer to Massachusetts General Laws Chapter 195, Section 16, as amended.

Death certificate must be filed with application.

Give motor vehicle identification number.

Status of applicant includes the following:

surviving spouse, child, grandchild, parent, brother, sister, niece, nephew, aunt or uncle if of full age and legal capacity and inhabitant of the Commonwealth of Massachusetts.

Notice Regarding Massachusetts Estate Taxes

You may need to file a Massachusetts Estate Tax Return and a Massachusetts Fiduciary Income Tax Return, especially if the decedent owned an interest in real estate, or if the decedent had more than $100 of income received after the date of death.

You may need to file a Massachusetts Estate Tax Return (Form M-706) in order to obtain a release of lien (Form M-792) on this real estate.

You may need to file a Massachusetts Fiduciary Income Tax Return (Form 2) to report income of more than $100 received after the date of death.

You should contact the Massachusetts Estate Tax Bureau for information and assistance regarding the estate tax law (617-727-4448) or the fiduciary income tax law (617-727-4305).

Form 3

Commonwealth of Massachusetts
The Trial Court

_____ Division   Probate and Family Court Department   Docket No. _____

Probate of Will With/Without Sureties

Name of Decedent _____

Domicile at Death _____
                  (Street and No.)   (City or Town)   (County)   (Zip)

Date of Death _____

Name and address of Petitioner(s) _____

_____ Status_____

Heirs at law or next of kin of deceased including surviving spouse:

Name	**Residence** (minors and incompetents must be so designated)	**Relationship**

That said deceased left a will — and codicil(s) — herewith presented, wherein your petitioner(s) is/are named
execut _____
and wherein the testat _____ had requested that your petitioner(s) be exempt from giving surety on his/her/their
bond(s).

☐ The petitioner(s) hereby certif ____ that a copy of this document, along with a copy of the decedent's death
certificate has been sent by certified mail to the **Department of Public Welfare, P.O. Box 86, Essex Station,
Boston, Massachusetts 02112.**
Wherefore your petitioner(s) pray(s) that said will — and codicil(s) — may be proved and allowed, and that
he/she/they be appointed execut ____ thereof, with/without surety on his/her/their bond(s) and certif ____ under the
penalties of perjury that the statements herein contained are true to the best of his/her/their knowledge and belief.

Date_____   Signature(s)_____

_____

The undersigned hereby assent to the foregoing petition and to the allowance of the will without testimony.

_____   _____
_____   _____
_____   _____
_____   _____

DECREE

All persons interested having been notified in accordance with the law or having assented and no objections being
made thereto, it is decreed that said instrument(s) be approved and allowed as the last will and testament of said
deceased, and that said petitioner(s): _____
of_____
and_____ of_____
_____ be appointed
execut_____ thereof, first giving bond with_____ sureties for the due performance of said trust.

Date_____   _____
                                  JUSTICE OF THE PROBATE AND FAMILY COURT

CJ-P2 (8/92)   89

For Petitioner:

_____

_____

Tel. No. _____

For Respondent:

_____

_____

Tel. No. _____

Publication in the _____

_____

Docket No. _____

Probate of Will

With/Without Sureties

Petition — Decree

Filed _____ 19_____

Citation Issued _____ 19_____

Returnable _____ 19_____

Allowed _____ 19_____

Recorded Vol. _____ Page _____

Instructions

Refer to Massachusetts General Laws Chapter 192.

COMMONWEALTH OF MASSACHUSETTS.
THE TRIAL COURT

To the Honorable the Justices of the Probate and Family Court, in and for the County of Norfolk:

It being inconvenient for . . . .

to discharge the duty of execut   of — trustee under — the last will and testament of

. . . .

late of . . . . .in said County of . . . .,

deceased, ... do hereby decline that trust.

Dated this . . . . .day of 19

. . . .

No. ....

. . . .

DECLINATION.

. . . .

Filed .... , 19   .

Commonwealth of Massachusetts
The Trial Court
Probate and Family Court Department

_____ Division   Docket No. _____

General Assent

Estate of _____

In the matter of _____

I, _____ of _____

_____

being a party interested in the above matter hereby consent to the allowance of the same by the Probate and Family

Court for this County and request that the same be granted without further notice.

_____   _____   _____
Witness   Date   Signature

Release Of All Demands And Assent To Account

In the matter of _____

In consideration of _____ dollars

paid by _____ , the receipt whereof is hereby acknowledged

I, _____ of _____

_____

do hereby release and forever discharge the said _____

from all debts and liabilities whatsoever which I now have for or on account of the estate of

_____

_____

and I further consent to the allowance of the petition — account — appointment described above.

_____   _____   _____
Witness   Date   Signature

CJ-P 21 (8/88)

Commonwealth of Massachusetts
The Trial Court
_____ Division   **Probate and Family Court Department**   Docket No. _____

Appointment of Agent

I, _____ of _____
(Street and No.)

_____ appoint
(City or Town)   (County)   (State)   (Zip)

_____ of

_____
(Street and No.)   (City or Town)   (County)   (Zip)

as my agent and I do stipulate and agree that the service of any legal process against me as administrator/admin-

istratrix —executor/executrix — trustee — of the estate of _____

late of _____
(Street and No.)

_____
(City or Town)   (County)   (Zip)

or as guardian/conservator of _____

of _____
(Street and No.)   (City or Town)   (County)   (Zip)

or against me in my individual capacity of any action founded upon or arising out of my acts or omissions as such
fiduciary if made on said agent, shall have like effect as if made on me personally within said Commonwealth.

Date_____   Signature_____

Signed in the presence of _____

_____
WITNESS

Acceptance

I, _____ accept the above appointment.

_____
(Street and No.)   (City or Town)   (State)   (Zip)

Commonwealth of Massachusetts
The Trial Court
_____ Division **Probate and Family Court Department**   Docket No. _____

Military Affidavit

Estate of _____

late of _____
      (street and no.)   (city or town)

_____ Date of Death _____
(county)   (zip)

   In the matter of the — petition — complaint of _____

_____

account of _____

_____

   I, _____ of_____
                                                    (street and no.)

_____
(city or town)   (county)   (zip)

on oath depose and say that none of the — heirs-at-law — parties interested — in said petition — complaint —
account — are in the military service of the United States or citizens of the United States in the military service
of its allies.

_____

on oath depose and say that _____
_____
_____
_____

heirs-at-law — parties interested — in said petition — complaint — account — are in the military service of the United
States or citizens of the United States in the military service of its allies.

_____

on oath depose and say that I am unable to determine whether or not _____
_____
_____
_____
_____

heirs-at-law — parties interested — in said petition — complaint — account — are in the military service of the United
States or citizens of the United States in the military service of its allies.

Signed under the penalties of perjury this _____ day of _____ 19_____ .

Signature _____

CJ-P 148 (1/89)

Commonwealth of Massachusetts
The Trial Court

_____ Division   **Probate and Family Court Department**   **Docket No.** _____

Administration With/Without Sureties

Name of Decedent _____

Domicile at Death _____
            (Street and No.)   (City or Town)   (County)   (Zip)

Date of Death _____

Name and address of Petitioner(s) _____

_____

_____ Status _____

Heirs at law or next of kin of deceased including surviving spouse:

Name	Residence (minors and incompetents must be so designated)	Relationship
_____	_____	_____
_____	_____	_____
_____	_____	_____
_____	_____	_____
_____	_____	_____
_____	_____	_____

☐ The petitioner(s) hereby certif ____ that a copy of this document, along with a copy of the decedent's death certificate has been sent by <u>certified mail</u> to the **Department of Public Welfare, P.O. Box 86, Essex Station, Boston, Massachusetts 02112.**

Petitioner(s) pray(s) that he/she/they or some other suitable person_____

of_____ in the County of _____ be appointed administrat _____ of said estate with/without surety on his/her/their bond(s) and certif_____ under the penalties of perjury that the foregoing statements are true to the best of his/her/their knowledge and belief.

Date_____   Signature(s)_____

                                                  _____

The undersigned hereby assent to the foregoing petition.

_____   _____

_____   _____

_____   _____

DECREE

All persons interested having been notified in accordance with the law or having assented and no objections being made thereto, it is decreed that _____

of_____ in the

County of_____ be appointed administrat _____ of said estate first giving bond

with_____ sureties for the due performance of said trust.

Date_____   _____

                                                    JUSTICE OF THE PROBATE AND FAMILY COURT

CJ-P1 (8/92)

For Petitioner:

_____

_____

Tel. No._____

For Respondent:

_____

_____

Tel. No._____

Publication in the_____

_____

Docket No._____

Administration

With/Without Sureties

Petition — Decree

Filed_____ 19_____

Citation Issued_____ 19_____

Returnable_____ 19_____

Allowed_____ 19_____

Recorded Vol._____ Page_____

Instructions

Refer to Massachusetts General Laws Chapter 193, Section 1.

1. Assents of **all** persons required for **filing** Administrations Without Sureties.

2. Petitioner must be a party in interest or have assent of at least **one** interested person for **filing** with sureties.

3. Certified copy of appointment of a fiduciary is required if appointment is not in same Court.

4. Strike words "or some other suitable person" if this is a petition for Administration Without Sureties.

Commonwealth of Massachusetts
The Trial Court
_____ Division   **Probate and Family Court Department**   **Docket No.** _____

Probate Of Will - Administration With The Will Annexed
With - Without - Sureties

Name of Decedent _____

Domicile at Death _____
                (street and no.)   (city or town)

_____ Date of Death _____
       (county)   (zip)

Name and address of Petitioner(s)_____

_____ Status _____

Heirs at law or next of kin of deceased including surviving spouse:

Name	Residence (minors and incompetents must be so designated)	Relationship

That said deceased left a will — and codicil(s) — herewith presented, wherein_____
_____ is named executor/executrix but has — declined to
serve — died — become incapacitated.

☐ The petitioner(s) hereby certif____that a copy of this document, along with a copy of the decedent's death
certificate has been sent by <u>certified mail</u> to the **Department of Public Welfare, P.O. Box 86, Essex Station,
Boston, Massachusetts 02112.**

Wherefore your petitioner(s) pray(s) that said will—and codicil(s) —may be proved and allowed, and that he/she/they
or some other suitable person_____
of _____
   (street and no.)   (city or town)   (county)   (zip)

be appointed administrator/administratrix with the will annexed, — with — without — sureties on his/her bond,
and certif____ under the penalties of perjury that the statements herein contained are true to the best of his/her/
their knowledge and belief.

Date_____   Signature_____

The undersigned hereby assent to the foregoing petition and to the allowance of the will without testimony.

_____   _____
_____   _____
_____   _____

DECREE
All persons interested having been notified in accordance with the law or having assented and no objections
being made thereto, it is decreed that said instrument(s) be approved and allowed as the last will and testament
of said deceased, and that_____ of _____
_____ in the County of _____
be appointed administrat _____with the will annexed of said estate first giving bond, with _____ sureties,
for the due performance of said trust.

Date_____   _____ 101

CJ-P 3 (8/92)   Justice of the Probate and Family Court

For Petitioner:

_____

_____

Tel No. _____

For Respondent:

_____

_____

Tel. No. _____

Publication in the _____

_____

Docket No. _____

Probate Of Will
Administration
With The Will Annexed
With/Without Sureties
Petition — Decree

Filed _____ 19____

Citation Issued _____ 19____

Returnable _____ 19____

Allowed _____ 19____

Recorded Vol. _____ Page _____

Instructions

Refer to Massachusetts General Laws Chapter 193, Section 7.

Commonwealth of Massachusetts
The Trial Court
_____ Division   Probate and Family Court Department   Docket No. _____

Special Administration

Name of Decedent _____

Domicile at Death _____
               (street and no.)   (city or town)

_____ Date of Death_____
   (county)   (zip)

Name and address of Petitioner(s)_____

_____ Status _____

Respectfully represent(s) that said decedent died possessed of goods and estate remaining to be administered, and that there is delay in securing the appointment of _____
_____ of the estate of said decedent by reason
of _____
_____

☐ The petitioner(s) hereby certif____ that a copy of this document, along with a copy of the decedent's death certificate has been sent by <u>certified mail</u> to the **Department of Public Welfare, P.O. Box 86, Essex Station, Boston, Massachusetts 02112.**

Wherefore your petitioner(s) pray(s) that he/she/they or some other suitable person: _____
of_____
                        (street and no.)

_____ may be appointed special
  (city or town)   (county)   (zip)

administrator/administratrix of said decedent and may be authorized to take charge of all the real estate of said decedent and to collect rents and make necessary repairs; and may be authorized to continue the business of the decedent for the benefit of his/her estate, and certif____ under the penalties of perjury that the statements herein contained are true to the best of his/her/their knowledge and belief.

Date_____   Signature_____

The undersigned hereby assent to the foregoing petition.

_____   _____
_____   _____
_____   _____
_____   _____

DECREE

All persons interested having been notified in accordance with the law or having assented and no objections being

made thereto, it is decreed that _____ of _____

_____ in the County of_____ be appointed

administrat_____ of said estate, first giving bond with_____ sureties, for the due performance of said trust.

Date_____   _____
                                             Justice of the Probate and Family Court

CJ-P 8 (8/92)

For Petitioner:

_____

_____

Tel No. _____

For Respondent:

_____

_____

Tel. No. _____

Publication in the _____

_____

Docket No. _____

Special Administration

Petition — Decree

Filed _____ 19____

Citation Issued _____ 19____

Returnable _____ 19____

Allowed _____ 19____

Recorded Vol. _____ Page _____

Instructions

Refer to Massachusetts General Laws Chapter 193, Section 10.

The Trial Court

_____ Division **Probate and Family Court Department** Docket No. _____

( ) **without**

Bond of _____ ( ) **with Personal Surety**
_____(type of fiduciary)

( ) **with Corporate Surety**

Name of Estate_____

Name and Address of Fiduciary_____

_____

Estimated Real Estate_____ Estimated Personal Estate_____

Penal Sum of Bond, (if applicable) _____

I, We, the undersigned fiduciary accept appointment as_____
and stand bound — in the aforesaid penal sum — with the undersigned surety or sureties — (if applicable) to perform the statutory conditions of said bond and declare the above estimate to be to my — our best knowledge and
belief.

Date_____   _____
                                                              Signature of Fiduciary — Principal

(complete below only if this is a bond with personal sureties)

We, the undersigned, as sureties, stand bound jointly and severally in the aforesaid penal sum to perform the
statutory condition.

Personal Surety's Name and Address_____

_____

Signature _____

Personal Surety's Name and Address_____

_____

Signature _____

The above sureties are in my opinion sufficient.

_____   _____   _____
          Signature   Office   City or Town

(complete below only if this is a Surety Company Bond)

We, the undersigned surety company, a corporation duly organized by law under the state of
_____ and having a usual place of business in _____
_____
                                                  (Massachusetts address)
stand bound as surety, in the aforesaid penal sum, to perform the statutory condition.

_____ by_____
          Corporate Surety (name)   Signature and Title

_____ , ss.   _____ 19_____ examined and approved.

                                                      _____
CJ-P 26 (1/89)   Justice-Assistant-Register-of The Probate and Family Court

No.

FIDUCIARY BOND

Filed _____ 19 _____

Approved _____ 19 _____

INSTRUCTIONS

Reference — Massachusetts General Laws Chapter 205, Section 1

This form covers the following fiduciaries:

Administrator — Administratrix

Public — de bonis non — with the will annexed — de bonis with the will annexed

Executor — Executrix

Trustee under a will or written instrument

Temporary and permanent conservator, guaridan to minor, mentally ill or mentally retarded persons

Receiver of the property of an absentee

Sureties must be residents of Massachusetts or in the case of a Surety Company have a usual place of business in Massachusetts.

AFFIDAVIT OF DOMICILE

Commonwealth of Massachusetts

_____, ss.   _____, 19__

_____, being duly sworn, deposes and says that he/she resides at _____, and is the Executor of the Estate of _____, deceased, who died on the _____ day of _____, 19__, that at the time of his/her death the domicile of said decedent was at _____, _____, _____ County, Commonwealth of Massachusetts; that said decedent resided at such address for _____ (   ) years, commencing in 19__; that said decedent last voted in the year 19__, at _____ County, Commonwealth of Massachusetts; that the decedent's most recent federal income tax return showed his/her legal residence as _____, _____, Massachusetts; that within three years prior to the decedent's death he/she was not a resident of another State; that the securities presented herewith, belonging to the decedent were physically located in the Commonwealth of Massachusetts, on the date of the decedent's death; that all debts and taxes and claims against the decedent's estate have been paid or are being provided for; that this affidavit is made for the purpose of securing the transfer of property owned by the decedent at the time of his death to a person legally entitled thereto under the laws of the decedent's domicile.

_____
, Executor

Then personally appeared the above named _____ and acknowledged the foregoing as her free and voluntary act.

_____
Notary Public
my commission expires:

_____ , 199__

_____
_____
_____

Re: _____
     _____

Dear Sir/Madam:

Please be advised that _____ passed away on _____ , 199__ (death certificate enclosed). As Executor/Administrator of this Estate, I am in need of the balance of this account as of the date of death.

Please send this information directly to me:

Additionally, please arrange to have this account closed and a check made payable to:

Estate of _____ , _____ , **Executor/Administrator**

Please forward this check directly to me at the address noted above.

Very truly yours,

_____
Executor/Administrator

Enclosure

_____ , 199__

_____
_____
_____

attn: Legal Processing Department

Re: _____

_____

Dear Sir/Madam:

Please be advised that _____passed away on _____, 199__ and we are presently in the process of collecting all assets owned by _____. I would appreciate your closing the mutual fund account maintained in the decedent's name, and opening a new account in the name of the Estate of _____.

To assist in processing this I am enclosing the following items:

1. Original Death Certificate for _____;

2. An election notice for federal income tax purposes;

3. Form W-9, Employer Identification Number for the Estate;

4. Certificate of Appointment of _____ as Executor/Executrix of the estate of _____.

If you have any questions, please contact me.

Very truly yours,

_____
Executor/Executrix

SIGNATURE GUARANTEED

By:_____
(signature)

_____
(printed name/title)

Form **SS-4** (Rev. December 1993) Department of the Treasury Internal Revenue Service	**Application for Employer Identification Number** (For use by employers, corporations, partnerships, trusts, estates, churches, government agencies, certain individuals, and others. See instructions.)	EIN OMB No. 1545-0003 Expires 12-31-96

Please type or print clearly.

1 Name of applicant (Legal name) (See instructions.)

2 Trade name of business, if different from name in line 1

3 Executor, trustee, "care of" name

4a Mailing address (street address) (room, apt., or suite no.)

5a Business address, if different from address in lines 4a and 4b

4b City, state, and ZIP code

5b City, state, and ZIP code

6 County and state where principal business is located

7 Name of principal officer, general partner, grantor, owner, or trustor – SSN required (See instructions.) ▶

8a Type of entity (Check only one box.) (See instructions.)

- ☐ Sole Proprietor (SSN) _____
- ☐ REMIC   ☐ Personal service corp.
- ☐ State/local government   ☐ National guard
- ☐ Other nonprofit organization (specify) _____
- ☐ Other (specify) ▶ _____
- ☐ Estate (SSN of decedent) _____
- ☐ Plan administrator–SSN _____
- ☐ Other corporation (specify) _____
- ☐ Federal government/military   ☐ Church or church controlled organization
- (enter GEN if applicable) _____
- ☐ Trust
- ☐ Partnership
- ☐ Farmers' cooperative

8b If a corporation, name the state or foreign country (if applicable) where incorporated ▶   State _____   Foreign country _____

9 Reason for applying (Check only one box.)

- ☐ Started new business (specify) ▶ _____
- ☐ Hired employees
- ☐ Created a pension plan (specify type) ▶ _____
- ☐ Banking purpose (specify) ▶ _____
- ☐ Changed type of organization (specify) ▶ _____
- ☐ Purchased going business
- ☐ Created a trust (specify) ▶ _____
- ☐ Other (specify) ▶ _____

10 Date business started or acquired (Mo., day, year) (See instructions.)

11 Enter closing month of accounting year. (See instructions.)

12 First date wages or annuities were paid or will be paid (Mo., day, year). **Note:** If applicant is a withholding agent, enter date income will first be paid to nonresident alien. (Mo., day, year) ▶

13 Enter highest number of employees expected in the next 12 months. **Note:** If the applicant does not expect to have any employees during the period, enter "0." ▶

Nonagricultural	Agricultural	Household

14 Principal activity (See instructions.)

15 Is the principal business activity manufacturing? ....   ☐ **Yes**   ☐ **No**
If "Yes," principal product and raw material used ▶

16 To whom are most of the products or services sold? Please check the appropriate box.   ☐ Business (wholesale)
☐ Public (retail)   ☐ Other (specify) ▶   ☐ N/A

17a Has the applicant ever applied for an identification number for this or any other business? ....   ☐ **Yes**   ☐ **No**
Note: If "Yes," please complete lines 17b and 17c.

17b If you checked the "Yes" box in line 17a, give applicant's legal name and trade name, if different than name shown on prior application.

Legal name ▶   Trade name ▶

17c Enter approximate date, city, and state where the application was filed and the previous employer identification number if known.

Approximate date when filed (Mo., day, year)	City and state where filed	Previous EIN

Under penalties of perjury, I declare that I have examined this application, and to the best of my knowledge and belief, it is true, correct, and complete. | Business Telephone number (include area code)

Name and title (Please type or print clearly.) ▶

Signature ▶   Date ▶

Note: Do not write below this line. For official use only.

Please leave blank ▶	Geo.	Ind.	Class	Size	Reason for applying

For Paperwork Reduction Act Notice, see attached instructions.   Form **SS-4** (Rev. 12-93)

H763
4W9012 1.000

113

AFFIDAVIT REGARDING FEDERAL ESTATE TAXES

I, _____, of _____,
_____, Massachusetts, Executor/Administrator of the Estate of
_____ who died on _____, 199_ a resident of
_____, _____ County, Massachusetts (the "Decedent"),
do under oath depose and say that the Decedent's gross estate as defined in IRC Section 2031
is less than $ 600,000 and accordingly no federal estate taxes are due and no federal estate tax
return will be filed for this estate.

Signed under the pains and penalties of perjury this_____ day of_____, 199_

_____

COMMONWEALTH OF MASSACHUSETTS

_____, ss. _____, 199_

Then personally appeared the above-named _____ and
made oath that the foregoing statement is true and acknowledged the foregoing to be her free
act and deed, before me,

_____
Notary Public
My commission expires:

Commonwealth of Massachusetts
The Trial Court
_____ Division   **Probate and Family Court Department**   Docket No. _____

SALE OF REAL ESTATE

TO THE HONORABLE JUSTICES OF THE PROBATE AND FAMILY COURT IN AND FOR THE COUNTY OF
_____ :

RESPECTFULLY represents _____
administrat _____ of the estate — execut _____ of the will — of _____
(late) of _____ ,
in the County of _____ , deceased, — testate — intestate —
that he/she/they gave bond for the faithful performance of his/her/their duties on _____ ,
19 _____ ; that said deceased was at the time of his/her decease the owner of certain real estate situated in
_____ , in the County of _____
bounded and described as follows:

_____
_____
_____
_____
_____
_____
_____
_____
_____

the same being — all — part — of the real estate of said deceased.

That it is for the advantage of all parties interested that the same be sold; that an advantageous offer for the purchase of said real estate has been made to the petitioner in the sum of _____ dollars.

I —We - certify that the estate of said deceased —does —does not - exceed $1000 in value.

WHEREFORE your petitioner(s) pray(s) that he/she/they may be authorized to sell said real estate of said deceased —at private sale in accordance with said offer or for a larger sum —at public auction upon the following terms:_____
_____

and that he/she/they may become the purchaser(s) of said real estate.

Date _____   _____

Date _____   _____

The undersigned, being all persons interested, hereby assent to the foregoing petition.

_____ _____   _____

_____   _____

CJ-P 76 (8/92)

Commonwealth of Massachusetts
The Trial Court

_____ Division   Probate and Family Court Department   Docket No. _____

I, We, _____

administrat _____ of the estate — execut _____ of the will — of _____

late of _____

in the County of _____ , deceased — testate — intestate —,

the petitioner(s) named in a petition dated_____and on file in said

County, praying for authority to sell certain real estate belonging to the estate of said deceased and therein described, do hereby certify under the penalties of perjury that the names of all persons known to – me – us as having or claiming any interest in said real estate derived from any deed or conveyance or mortgage by, through or under any of the – heirs – devisees of said deceased are as follows:

NAME	RESIDENCE	TITLE

Moreover, the petitioner(s) certif _____ that the Department of Public Welfare is an interested party in this matter due to:

☐ the filing of a written claim against the estate pursuant to M.G.L. ch. 118E, § 16A.

☐ the filing of a Notice of Claim pursuant to M.G.L. ch. 197, § 9(a).

and request(s) that notice of this petition be sent to the **Department of Public Welfare, P.O. Box 86, Essex Station, Boston, Massachusetts 02112.**

Date _____   _____

　　　　　　　　　　　　　　　　　Administrat _____ — Execut _____

_____ Division   **Probate and Family Court Department**   Docket No. _____

At a Probate and Family Court held at _____ , in and for said County of _____ ,
on the _____ day of _____ in the year of our Lord one thousand
nine hundred and _____ .

On the petition of _____
administrat _____ of the estate — execut _____ of the will — of _____ ___
late of _____ ,
in said County, deceased, —testate —intestate —praying for authority to sell certain real estate of said deceased
described in said petition —at public auction —at private sale, in accordance with the offer named in said
petition or for a larger sum, or at public auction, if he/she/they shall think best so to do; all persons interested
having —assented —been duly notified —and no person objecting thereto, it appearing that said offer is an
advantageous one and that the interest of all parties concerned will be best promoted by an acceptance of
said offer.

It is expedient to sell real estate of said deceased.

IT IS DECREED that the petitioner(s) be authorized to sell and convey —at public auction —at private sale,
upon the following terms:
_____
_____
_____

for the sum of _____
in accordance with said offer or for a larger sum, or at public auction — if he/she/they shall think best so
to do, the real estate of said deceased described as follows:
_____
_____
_____
_____
_____
_____
_____
_____
_____
_____
_____

The Commissioner of Corporations and Taxation has released —discharged —the lien on said real estate
—and it is further decreed that said petitioner(s) may become the purchaser(s) of said real estate.

_____
Justice of the Probate and Family Court

For Petitioner:

_____

_____

Tel. No. _____

For Respondent:

_____

_____

Tel. No. _____

Publication in the _____

Docket No. _____

Sale Of Real Estate

Administrator — Executor

Petition — Citation — Decree

Filed _____ 19____

Citation Issued _____ 19____

Returnable _____ 19____

Allowed _____ 19____

Decree Recorded Vol. _____ Page _____

Commonwealth of Massachusetts
The Trial Court
_____ Division   **Probate and Family Court Department**   **Docket No.** _____

Account

_____ Account of _____
_____ and _____
_____ as _____
(Specify type of fiduciary and name of estate)

This account is for the period of _____ _____ to _____
_____ inclusive.

Principal amounts received per Schedule A	$ _____
Principal payments and charges per Schedule B	$ _____
Principal balance invested per Schedule C	$ _____
Market value as of _____ per Schedule C (date)	$ _____
Income received per Schedule D	$ _____
Payments from income per Schedule E	$ _____
Income balance per Schedule F	$ _____

The United States Veterans' Administration is - is not - a party in interest to this account. The ward is - is not - a patient in a State Hospital.

I - We certify under the penalties of perjury that the within account is just and true.

Date _____

_____

_____

_____
Signature of Fiduciary

The undersigned, being _____ interested, having examined the foregoing account, request that the same may be allowed without further notice.

_____
_____
_____
_____
_____

For Petitioner:

_____

_____

Tel No. _____

For Respondent:

_____

_____

Tel. No. _____

Publication in the _____

_____

Docket No. _____

Account

Filed _____ 19_____

Citation Issued _____ 19_____

Returnable _____ 19_____

Allowed _____ 19_____

Recorded Vol. _____ Page _____

Instructions

Refer to Massachusetts General Laws Chapter 206.
(Sugested format for Schedules and use continuation sheets as needed)

SCHEDULE A   shall contain the amount of personal property and with respect to a trustee, guardian or conservator, also the amount of real property, per inventory or balance of principal according to next prior account, and amounts received on account of principal or gains from the sale of any property.

SCHEDULE B   shall contain amounts paid out and charges on account of principal, losses and distributions of estates.

SCHEDULE C   shall contain the investment of the balance of such account with market values of all assets separately stated. A final account of fiduciary shall contain no balance in this Schedule. Schedule C requires both appraised (book) and market values (P.R. 29A).

SCHEDULE D   **trustees** only shall report balance of income according to next prior account and amounts received on account of income.

SCHEDULE E   **trustees** only shall report payments chargeable to income.

SCHEDULE F   **trustees** only shall report balance of income.

Commonwealth of Massachusetts
The Trial Court
_____ Division   **Probate and Family Court Department**   Docket No._____

Judgment

Estate of_____

At the Probate and Family Court held at _____

in and for said County, on_____, 199___.

The _____ account(s) of _____,

_____, _____

of the estate of _____

(late) of _____

(street and no.)   (city or town)   (county)   (zip)

The said account(s) of said, _____

_____ having been presented for allowance, and certified by the accountant — and the guardian ad litem — and all persons interested — having been duly notified — having consented thereto in writing, and no objections being made thereto, and the same having been examined and considered by the Court.

It is ordered and adjudged that said account(s) be allowed.

Date_____

_____
Justice of the Probate and Family Court

CJ-P 38 (1/89)

RECEIPT FOR DISTRIBUTION

I, _____, of _____ Massachusetts hereby acknowledge receipt of $ _____ from the Estate of _____, _____, Administrator, as a partial distribution from the Estate. In consideration of said distribution the undersigned hereby agrees as follows:

1. That this distribution is made upon the condition that the assets of the estate of _____ remaining in the hands of the Administrator after this distribution, shall be sufficient to pay all of the debts and claims properly payable by the Administrator, to reimburse him for his expenses and to pay any federal, state or local tax payable by the executor, and

2. That I will indemnify the Administrator and hold him harmless from any debts, claims, expenses or taxes properly payable by him to the extent, if any, that the assets remaining in the said estate after this distribution shall be insufficient therefore, but not in excess of the amount of said distribution, and

3. That I, without further notice, hereby assent to any and all accounts of said _____ as Administrator of the Estate of _____ that reflects said distribution to me.

Dated this _____ day of _____, 199___

_____

Social Security No. _____

Index

Account, 68, 121
Accounts, 61, 63
Administration, 30
Administrator, 27
Affidavit of Domicile, 43, 107
Allowance, 64, 65
Anatomical gifts, 12
Ancillary administration, 59
Appeal of allowed account, 67
Appointment of agent, 24, 95
Appointment, 14
Assents, 66
Assets, 38, 41
Attorney, 10, 11
Automobile, 12

Balance, 62
Bank accounts, 38, 40
Bond with sureties, 33
Bond without sureties, 34
Bond, 19, 28, 35, 105

Charities, 65
Checklist, 79
Citation, 19, 20, 28, 29
Claims, 55
Closing accounts, 39
Closing probate docket, 61
Collecting assets and expenses, 39
Contesting an account, 66
Creditors, 55

Death certificate, 29
Debts, 55
Declination, 22
Delivery of will, 11
Distribution of Intestate property, 73

Estate tax, 49, 57, 66
Expenditures, 62
Expenses, 55

Federal estate tax, 49, 51, 57, 115
Filing fees, 19, 28
Forms, 83

Form 1, 15, 85
Form 2, 16, 87
Form 3, 21, 89
Form 4, 22, 91
Form 5, 23, 93
Form 6, 24, 95
Form 7, 15, 97
Form 8, 30, 99
Form 9, 31, 101
Form 10, 32, 103
Form 11, 35, 105
Form 12, 43, 107
Form 13, 44, 109
Form 14, 45, 111
Form 15, 46, 113
Form 16, 51, 115
Form 17, 54, 117
Form 18, 68, 121
Form 19, 72, 123
Form 20, 75, 125
Funeral, 12

General Assent, 23, 93
Glossary, 77
Guardian Ad Litem, 65

Identification Number, 41
Insurance, 42
Inventory, 37
Investments, 38

Judgment, 66, 72, 123

Legacies, 73, 74
Legal requirements, 13
Lost or misplaced wills, 11

Mailing, 64
Massachusetts estate tax, 58
Military affidavit, 25, 66, 97
Minors, 75
Mutual Funds, 45

Non residents, 59
Notices, 20, 29

Ownership of property, 10

Paying bills, 40
Personal estate, 37
Petition, 18, 19, 28
Probate bond, 33
Probate with a will, 17
Probate without will, 27
Probate, 9
Publication, 64
Purchase agreement, 49

Real estate, 37, 47, 48, 54, 74
Receipt for distribution, 75, 125
Receipts, 62

Safe deposit box, 12
Sale agreement, 49
Sale of real estate, 117
Small estates, 13
Social Security, 42
Stock Brokerage accounts, 40
Stocks and bonds, 38

Transmittal letter, 66

Valuation, 47
Voluntary Administration, 14, 87
Voluntary Executor, 14, 85

Will, 19

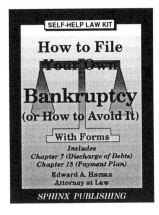
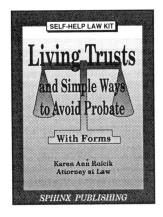